P9-AOU-844

With a Servant Heart

Perspectives on women in leadership

WMU, SBC
Birmingham, Alabama

Woman's Missionary Union, SBC
P. O. Box 830010
Birmingham, AL 35283-0010

© 1992 Woman's Missionary Union

All rights reserved. Third printing 1996
Printed in the United States of America

Dewey Decimal Classification: 266.007
Subject Headings: LEADERSHIP
                  WOMAN'S MISSIONARY UNION—
                  HANDBOOKS, MANUALS, ETC.
                  WOMEN IN CHURCH WORK
                  WOMEN—BIBLICAL TEACHING

Scripture references followed by NIV are taken from the *Holy Bible: New International Version,* © 1978 by the International Bible Society. Used by permission of Zondervan Bible Publishers.

Scripture references followed by KJV are taken from the *Holy Bible,* King James Version.

Scripture references followed by TLB are taken from *The Living Bible Paraphrased,* © 1971 by Tyndale House Publishers, Wheaten, IL. Used by permission.

Scripture references followed by NASB are taken from the *New American Standard Bible,* © The Lockman Foundation, 1960, 1962, 1963, 1968, 1971, 1972, 1973, 1975, 1977. Published by Holman Bible Publishers, Nashville. Used by permission.

With a Servant Heart is the resource for the Leadership Skills Diploma Plan for Women in the Christian Growth Study Plan (formerly Church Study Course). For information about receiving credit, call (615) 251-2525.

ISBN: 1-56309-048-1

W923125•0496•1M3

contents

Introduction

"We're following the leader, the leader, the leader,
We're following the leader, wherever she may go."

Oh, that leadership were that easy! But then it would require no special expertise, and we wouldn't need a book about it. On the other hand, hundreds of books have been written on the topic of leadership, many available in your closest bookstore.

Why, then, another book on the subject? One reason, obviously, is that WMU focuses on leadership training through our organizations, and anyone who has served on a nominating committee knows how needed this emphasis is. It is becoming increasingly difficult to fill places of leadership, not only in Woman's Missionary Union organizations, but in any area of service in the local church or association.

The fact of the matter is that there is a wealth of leadership potential not yet tapped in our churches. If you sought affirmation of this fact from these "undiscovered" leaders, however, they would quickly assure you that they do not have the capability nor the qualities of a leader. They have never done it before, and they are quite confident they couldn't if they tried!

After observing a teacher with a group of third graders, I asked, "How do you account for the productive, happy work of the group?"

"Oh, I don't know. I like what I do and I love this group. It just sort of 'happens.'"

But for many of us, leadership does not "happen" so easily. Just feeling good about your job and loving your group is not enough.

Effective strategies come more naturally for some than for others, but even the most talented among us can benefit by setting out to master the art of leading.

"So leaders are made, not born then?" you ask.

Watch a group of preschoolers at play. You will no doubt observe that at least one child is "in charge," curious about everything going on, organizing the others, making decisions, giving orders. In one such group I commented to the teacher, "I see you have a good helper here in

Grace." The teacher's response was classic: "I think it's just the other way around!"

Revisit that same group of children a few years later. Is Grace still the "natural" leader? Maybe. For if she has practiced a variety of tactics in her search to become a strong leader, she will also have discovered that some strategies are more productive than others in maintaining a leadership role. If, however, the early bent toward leading was more manipulation and power than true leadership, her influence may no longer be so strong. Children are wise beyond their years in evaluating the motives of their peers. Over time, other children, perhaps quieter, less aggressive, may have emerged as the true leaders. The "becoming" of a leader is an interesting study!

Suppose, however, I have never been a "Grace," nor have I been even a "late bloomer" in leadership roles. Now, I am an adult, and count myself a confirmed follower.

First of all, there is nothing inferior about being a good follower. Don't dismiss any leadership ability, however, just because you have never been an elected officer of an organization. Have you ever taught a child to tie a shoe? Or to ride a bicycle? Have you ever persuaded someone to participate in a mission action project? Or provided an example to others in your faithful prayers for missionaries? If so, then, you have experienced *leadership*. Everyone can be a leader!

All God's children have special gifts which equip us to lead others. These gifts are not for our glory, but to bring honor to our Heavenly Father, "that they may see your good works and glorify the Father." He is constantly challenging and equipping us to do more for Him.

If you desire to be a more courageous follower of Christ, to risk in order to be obedient in servant leadership, then this book will tell you how. You have mentors of the highest rank in the contributors to this volume.

WMU called on six uniquely talented women to write this book on leadership skills for women. Their varied backgrounds, education, and experiences gave them different perspectives on leadership and how women lead. After several initial planning meetings, four of the six convened to tentatively outline the book and decide who would write the various chapters.

If the seed for their book was planted in the earlier discussions, this meeting was the first time when their seedling pushed through the soil and saw the light of day. They weren't sure when they left that the struggling plant would survive. Would the concept work? How would they handle differences in style and opinion among six authors? Would there be too much repetition? Did they really have anything worthwhile to say?

They did, and *With a Servant Heart* is the fruit of their labors. Their concept was to introduce a group of women, character studies who embodied various leadership styles and attitudes which would be addressed in the book. Barbara Joiner was chosen for that assignment; in her first chapter, she introduces a fictional group of women who make up a church WMU council. After meeting each of the women, their story is interrupted by the rest of the book which they study along with the readers. In chapter nine, Barbara shows how each woman responded to a different chapter in the text. Barbara's two chapters form a short story interrupted by the seven interior chapters.

Barbara Joiner is a frequent contributor to WMU publications and the author of three books, most recently *Count It All Joy*. A native of Alabama, Barbara is a popular speaker and active Acteens leader. A graduate of the University of Alabama, she is married and has two daughters and two grandchildren.

Susan Shaw wrote the chapters which give a biblical basis for servant leadership and offer a scriptural view of women as servant leaders. A sports enthusiast in her spare time, Susan is assistant professor of Christian ministries at George Fox College in Newberg, Oregon. A native of Rome, Georgia, she is a graduate of Berry College and Southern Baptist Theological Seminary.

Florida WMU Executive Director Barbara Curnutt is a native of San Antonio, Texas. She authored the two chapters on nurturing future leaders and one's image as a leader. Barbara is a graduate of Texas Tech University, Lubbock.

Alabama WMU Executive Director Beverly Sutton was assigned to write a chapter defining leadership. She titled her contribution, "What am I doing leading this parade? I didn't even plan to march!" That sums up what the group agreed was a problem for women in leadership: many women do not view their skills as those necessary for leadership roles. Beverly's chapter debunks that myth and other myths of leadership. Beverly is a native of Austin, Texas, and a graduate of the University of Mary Hardin-Baylor and Southwestern Baptist Theological Seminary.

Katharine Bryan, Executive Director-Treasurer of Tennessee WMU provided the chapter on varying leadership styles as well as the questions for thought at the end of chapters two through eight.

Katharine is a native of Nashville, Tennessee, and a graduate of Carson-Newman College and Southwestern Baptist Theological Seminary.

Finally, Bobbie Patterson authored the chapter on the dynamics of leadership. A native of Washington, D.C., Bobbie is a graduate of Carson-Newman College and Southern Baptist Theological Seminary. She is associate executive director for WMU, SBC, and became a minister's wife while working on *With a Servant Heart*.

Each of these women contributed a unique perspective on leadership. Among them, they have more than 100 years of leadership experience in missions on the local, association, state, and national levels. In their own ways, they model servant leadership with deep commitment, unquestioned integrity, and strong, abiding faith in God who calls each person, man or woman, to lead with a servant heart.

Dellanna O'Brien
Executive Director
Woman's Missionary Union, SBC

Take me to your leader
Barbara Joiner

---♡---

Anna Smith had just been elected Woman's Missionary Union director for Merrymount Baptist Church. Heady with power, she called a meeting of all the current WMU officers and age-level leaders. She could hardly wait to see who she would be directing and prodding and leading during the coming year.

Anna had never served as WMU director before. Mrs. Ada Palmer had held that position since Anna was a child. What Mrs. Palmer led or how, Anna did not know. "Nobody else would take it," Mrs. Palmer always explained. When Mrs. Palmer finally put her foot down—in the nursing home—someone else *had* to take it. Anna was elected. Merrymount Baptist Church was not prepared for Anna. She took the job and ran with it. Twelve months later everybody in the church had witnessed a whirlwind; a leader had come to power!

Anna loved all phases of leadership. She excelled in administration. She mapped out plans and strategies in great detail. She delegated responsibilities with a keen perception of who could do what.

Merrymount WMU had been muddling along, but now they had a dynamo who moved them to action, pushed them to get involved, and whipped them into shape.

Anna exuded raw leadership ability. In addition, she was a quick study. She attended associational leadership training, however, the conference was poorly taught. Anna recognized that. Then she went to state leadership training. The conference was led by an exceptional woman who was also an excellent teacher. Anna recognized that as well. She was challenged to read and study, and she followed through. Experimentation added to her leadership abilities. Anna knew she was a leader. She also realized that she craved the leadership role and was autocratic in her style.

When Anna called the meeting of WMU leaders in her church, she was aware of the past history of missions at Merrymount. In her mind, the top priority was to make missions an integral part of the entire church program, but first she wanted to really know what manner of women led in her WMU organizations. The first surprise was that only seven women including herself attended the called meeting. Anna recognized that her power was not yet established. "Plans must be made to get things under control," she thought. The next surprise was the seven women were not lesser versions of herself. Their styles of leadership varied as much as did their physical appearances.

Meet *Nancy Carter*, excellent Mission Friends leader, young wife and mother of two small children. Nancy had served on the leadership committee which nominated WMU officers and before she realized it, she had agreed to be the WMU Mission Study director for the coming year. Nancy had absolutely no experience in leading women in missions. She had served as Mission Friends leader; she taught children and taught them well.

2

However, the former Mission Study director, Mary Higgins, had been an excellent role model for Nancy. Together, they had attended training the state WMU provided. Mary encouraged Nancy and prayed for her. Nancy was becoming an excellent leader. Though not forceful or aggressive, she was easy to work with and was a diligent worker.

Nancy's first order of business was to sit down with Mary and to learn as much as she could from her. Nancy secured a planning calendar and a notebook. She began sketching in important dates: council meetings, annual planning meeting, Home and Foreign Mission Studies, weeks of prayer.

Mary also clued Nancy in on the women she would be working with on the WMU council. Nancy knew most of the women, but she listened to the wise advice and the different perspective that Mary gave her. She realized that her relationship skills were deficient. "I must work on this area," she vowed to herself.

Nancy was fortunate that Mary had agreed to continue working as a project leader to help Nancy—at least the first year. Mary would be an active participant in planning and praying. However, because of increased family responsibilities, an invalid mother who had come to live with Mary, she felt that she needed to pass the primary leadership role to someone else. She would continue to be as involved as her time would allow her to be. Mary knew that mission study was in capable hands, for more than anything else Nancy Carter wanted to serve the Lord with all her heart and soul and mind.

Judy Nelson had taken early retirement from a large bank. Judy had eagerly accepted the position of Baptist Women director; she was excited about her responsibilities. Active for many years in a night Baptist Women's organization, Judy was steeped in missions.

When her group studied a book on spiritual gifts, Judy discovered that her major gift was leadership. In fact, she had blown the lid off leadership, scoring a perfect ten. She went back to check the authenticity of her answers. Had she been completely honest?

Setting and achieving goals is important to me. Judy had marked "highly characteristic; this is definitely true for me." Judy knew this was the correct answer. She had always set goals for herself, even as a child, and she made every effort to reach the goals she set for herself.

Accomplishing something worthwhile takes great effort. Again Judy knew this was highly characteristic of herself. She had always given her very best if she believed a project was worthy of her attention.

I like to see all the pieces of a problem come together. Being a problem solver had advanced Judy in her career as a business woman. At church, Judy had taken the lead in missions fairs, banquets, World Mission Conferences. She had a major role in revising the personnel policies of the church; a complete personnel manual was designed. Judy could make things happen—neatly and completely.

I consider myself to be a hard worker. Everybody considered Judy a hard worker. She had gone from bank teller to vice president in charge of personnel because she was a hard worker. She worked hard in church and at home; she worked hard at being a good wife, mother and friend. Judy thought everybody did.

Completing a job is important to me. The job was not done until it was complete—that was Judy's motto. When Judy was a child, her father had said, "Winners never quit and quitters never win." One of the rules at home was "Finish what you start."

No mistakes had been made on that test. Judy had the qualities of

leadership. She read with deep satisfaction other qualities that leaders possess:
— interested in organization and delegation
— confident in standing before others
— ability to see needs
— giving attention to detail
— concerned about directions that are according to the "purposes and will of God."

Judy had all the equipment needed to lead and lead well. In addition, she had a deep commitment to the Lord and to missions.

Patsy Everheart was the sweetest, dearest woman in Merrymount Baptist Church. Everybody who knew Patsy loved her. When Patsy was elected WMU Mission Support director, she smiled and hugged everybody and said, "What do you mean; do you really want me? Do you think I can do it? Will all of you help me?"

Patsy had been elected to many offices during her life. She accepted graciously, but she held her elected positions very loosely. Most of her offices were honorary. Some, however, were not. She was scolded on occasion. Her big blue eyes would fill with tears, some of which would slide slowly down her cheeks. The scolder nearly always ended up apologizing. Some even accepted the blame for the failed assignment themselves.

When Patsy was asked to be WMU Mission Support director, she accepted that job, too. Everybody promised to help, and they did—when Patsy asked. But Patsy forgot.

She attended the annual planning meeting, but she made no preparation for the meeting. Somehow, the Week of Prayer for Foreign Missions slipped up on Patsy. In fact, she was doing her voluminous

5

Christmas shopping when she heard the carol "O Come All Ye Faithful" pealing out in the mall.

"I nearly died," she sobbed. "How did I let that wonderful week of prayer catch me by surprise? Why didn't you remind me?" she choked out. Anna tried to explain that she had called numerous times but she looked at the distraught Patsy and decided to let it go.

The Baptist Young Women president, *Jan Perkins*, had had it with Patsy, however. The BYW organization planned to use *Contempo* for their week of prayer observances, but Jan knew how important it was for the whole church to participate. At the very last minute, Jan had called Anna, and together they had prepared a brief presentation to be included in the midweek prayer service. The week of prayer had not gone completely unnoticed, but Jan knew it was too little too late.

Jan loved missions. She believed with all her heart that missions was the job of the church. She wanted her church to have a strong WMU as well as a strong churchwide missions program. Jan also knew that she had a head for organization. The BYW organization was exploding. Jan not only led, she developed other leaders. Several were ready for greater responsibility. In fact, Jackie had already agreed to be president in the coming year. God was calling Jan to other work. "Why not mission support?" Anna suggested.

Nell Mooney had been WMU secretary at Merrymount for 20 years. The handbook she compiled for the church each year and the current WMU Year Book stayed right with her Bible on the kitchen table. She lived by all three.

Nell prided herself on memorizing each new WMU Year Book. She knew the year's watchword before anybody else had heard it the first time. She could and often did sing every verse of the current hymn of the year. The emphasis for the year was burned into her mind. Her materials order was received at WMU headquarters months before the new products rolled off the presses. Every new publication, free or priced, was in her library. Both the Foreign Mission Board and the Home Mission Board were notified frequently to send new materials her way. She subscribed to the board's magazines; she wrote letters to the editor pointing out and explaining her appreciation or grievances.

Nell knew the exact number of countries where Southern Baptist missionaries serve. She could pronounce correctly the latest African entry. She often corrected the women at church.

Not only was Nell a fountain of missions knowledge, she eagerly attended every opportunity for training. Annually she journeyed to Ridgecrest or Glorieta for the WMU conference. She took tons of notes; she collected dozens of handouts. She attended conferences from dawn to dark. Nell never missed a meeting in her own state. She wrote regularly to several missionaries. Nell was sincere in this endeavor and prayed often for those with whom she corresponded.

Nell did indeed have a mind and heart for missions, but people skills were missing. She was sufficient unto herself. She rarely took other women with her to meetings. She attended planning sessions, but didn't really believe she was the one who needed to plan. She plodded right along with great knowledge but little know-how and absolutely no imagination.

Everybody agreed that Nell knew more about missions than anybody else at Merrymount Baptist Church, but who cared? Nell was uninspiring in her missions knowledge.

Anna gritted her teeth. "I must get to know Nell better, if I can stand it! There must be a way to reach her."

Sara Mullins was beginning her third year as Acteens director. She recognized that her leadership skills were not well developed; she wondered if they existed at all. But Sara was a praying woman and a hard worker. In addition, she recognized that she was surrounded by very capable women who knew their jobs, who would work with her and teach her. She had asked for their support and they had responded. They worked well as a team. Ideas were welcomed and weighed and put into action.

Sara spent days preparing for the Acteens annual planning meeting. She sought advice from all the Acteens leaders and from the Acteens officers. Sara suggested a luncheon for those participating in the planning meeting. She asked two capable women to handle the luncheon; they enlisted several Acteens to assist. Sara reminded them that she would be glad to do anything that needed to be done. All they had to do was ask.

The pastor was invited to the meeting. He was asked to listen to the plans for the year and to make any suggestions. He was also asked to pray a dedicatory prayer for the Acteens leaders and officers. Sara recognized the pastor was a strong supporter of WMU. The minister of youth with whom Sara worked hand-in-hand was also invited to attend. The meeting and luncheon were wonderful, inspirational and informative; it was a time of good fellowship. It set the stage for good planning all year. Council meetings were well-attended and productive. Working together, many exciting missions events and activities were planned and carried out. Acteens thrived. Members were added regularly. Nobody wanted to miss the wonderful things that were going on in Acteens.

Mary Ellen Thomas inherited her position in WMU from her mother, Mary Suellen, who had inherited it from her mother, Mary Ellen the first. It was a family tradition; the Thomas women had held every office listed in the *WMU Manual* and then some. It was said that Mary Ellen the first ran WMU with an iron hand. Mary Suellen did not have her mother's drive. Mary Ellen the second had even less get-up-and-go. But all three women hosted lovely parties. It was expected that they would be in WMU; the mantle was always passed.

Mary Ellen had been more languid than usual lately. Her children had flown the luxurious nest; both were now living in the city. Mary Ellen spent a lot of time on the phone and lot of time in the city. The rest of the time she cried. She was not handling the empty nest very well. Therefore, she was not handling anything very well. She had not planned her usual fall enlistment tea. Everybody had missed Mary Ellen's fantastic sour cream pound cake.

Mary Ellen feared that her daughter, Mary Catherine, would not return to their hometown. She also suspected that Mary Catherine did not participate in WMU and would not, under any circumstances, consider a leadership role. The mantle would not be passed. Even though her involvement had been minimal at times, Mary Ellen grieved over what she knew her daughter would be missing. Besides, what would her mother and grandmother have thought? They would roll over in their graves.

"I'm tired," Mary Ellen explained to her best friend, Elizabeth. "You should take a part in WMU. After all, our grandmothers were cousins. That makes you family."

Elizabeth smiled. "Mary Ellen, nobody can hold an enlistment tea like you. Is there more to WMU than that?" she asked.

Mary Ellen didn't know how to respond; she knew there was more to missions than she had experienced personally but she was worried

9

about Mary Catherine and she could not remember what job she had agreed to take this year. Was it enlistment again? She promised to go to Anna's called meeting. "I'll let you know what I find out," she promised Elizabeth.

There they are, Anna's WMU officers and leaders, along with a few friends and acquaintances. Let's go on with the book and meet them again in Chapter 9.

The paradox of servant leadership: A towel not a scepter

Susan Shaw

Giovanni Bernardone of Assisi spent much of his youth as a playboy. Nicknamed Francis by his father, the young man dreamed of glory as a soldier, but he was quickly disillusioned when he was captured. After one year as a prisoner of war, he returned home and fell seriously ill. These experiences led Francis to begin to question the values by which he lived. Bit by bit, he began to understand that God was calling him to minister to the outcasts of society.

When Francis began to sell his possessions in order to rebuild an old church, his father tried harshly to persuade him to forget his foolish notion. Even the bishop warned Francis not to go against his father's wishes. Francis responded by returning everything to his father, even his clothes, including the ones he was wearing at the moment.

"Now I will say only our Father which art in heaven," Francis replied.

He began to preach the gospel in nearby towns. Francis and his followers cared for lepers and spoke out against wealth and materialism. When the men returned from preaching and ministering to others, Francis washed their feet, fed them, and preached to them the joys of the kingdom. Their leader was also their servant.

Leadership has often been misunderstood as power or authority to dominate. The verb, *to lead*, actually means to show the way or direct

11

the course by going before or along with.

When missionary Lottie Moon first arrived in China in the mid 1800s, she continued to wear Western clothes; she considered the Chinese to be heathens. As she ministered there, however, she began to wear Chinese clothes and accept Chinese culture.

She wrote that missionaries "must be men and women of absolute self-consecration, ready to come down and live among the natives, to wear the Chinese dress, and live in Chinese houses, rejoicing in the footsteps of him who 'though he was rich, yet for our sakes he became poor,' . . . We do not ask people to come out to live in costly foreign style . . . barely touching the heathen world with the tips of their fingers but we ask them to come prepared to cast their lot with the natives."

What is leadership?

Leaders must be prepared first to be servants. Leadership is a gift from God, not an acquisition (Rom. 12:6 and 1 Cor. 12:28). As a gift, leadership carries with it a greater weight of responsibility. Paul notes that each person exercising his or her gift functions in much the same way as a part of the body carrying out its task. If one part fails to work, the entire body is affected.

In Ephesians 4:12, Paul explains that the purpose for God's gifts is for the building up of believers so that they will be able to carry out the ministries to which God has called them. Paul also admonishes believers in Romans 12 to use their gifts to their fullest potential.

The gift of leadership involves the ability to influence others and to empower them to move toward their goals in ministry. Christian leaders do not command and intimidate, rather they instruct and persuade in love as servants of God and servants of humanity. Jesus addresses this issue in Matthew 20:25-28:

You know that the rulers of the Gentiles lord it over them, and their high officials exercise authority over them. Not so with you. Instead, whoever wants to become great among you must be your servant, and whoever wants to be first must be your slave—just as the Son of Man did not come to be served, but to serve, and to give his life as a ransom for many (NIV).

Notice the contrasts in the leadership styles. The ruler is *over* those led, but the servant is *among*. The ruler *lords it over* and *exercises authority*, but the servant is commanded not to do so. The ruler tells, but the servant shows. The ruler coerces; the servant persuades.

In *Servant Leadership*, Robert Greenleaf contends that leadership

12

begins with the desire to serve. The servant-leader takes care to make sure that other needs are being met. The best test of servant leadership, he says, is: "Do those served grow as persons? Do they, *while being served*, become healthier, wiser, freer, more autonomous, more likely themselves to become servants?"

The best model of servant leadership is found in the life of Jesus. In the story of the temptations, Jesus struggles with the meaning of His mission. What kind of Messiah ought He to be? Contemporary Jewish thought held that the Messiah would be a political leader to liberate Israel. Jesus understood His role differently. His ministry would be built on the paradox of servant leadership.

In John 13, Jesus models servant leadership for the disciples. During the meal, Jesus takes a towel and a basin of water and begins to wash the disciples' feet. In so doing, He places Himself in the role of a servant, a role which, judging by Peter's reaction, makes the disciples very uncomfortable. But Jesus explains:

You call me 'Teacher' and 'Lord,' and rightly so, for that is what I am. Now that I, your Lord and Teacher, have washed your feet, you also should wash one another's feet. I have set you an example that you should do as I have done for you. I tell you the truth, no servant is greater than his master, nor is a messenger greater than the one who sent him (John 13:13-16 NIV).

Jesus demonstrates servant leadership throughout His ministry. He teaches with authority, but He teaches the way of the Kingdom as the way of the poor, the meek, the merciful, the pure, the peacemakers. He uses His power to heal and to meet needs. He shares His leadership by inviting others to join in His ministry.

Quoting a hymn of the ancient church, Paul describes Jesus as one "who being in very nature God, did not consider equality with God something to be grasped, but made himself nothing, taking the very nature of a servant, being made in human likeness. And being found in appearance as a man, he humbled himself and became obedient to death—even death on a cross!" (Phil. 2:6-8).

The pattern for servant leadership is found in the journey to the cross. When Jesus called His disciples, He asked them to leave everything and to become the servants of humanity. The Sermon on the Mount (Matt. 5-7) is filled with injunctions for God's Kingdom. Jesus contrasts the old and new, the rigors of the law against relationships of grace. He calls His followers to place concern for others over concern for self, to absorb evil rather than to pass it on, to serve God rather than keep laws.

The meaning of these lessons was not easily absorbed by the disciples who on a number of occasions fought over who would command authority in the group. In Mark 9:33-37, we find them arguing over who is the greatest. Jesus responds, "If anyone wants to be first, he must be the very last, and the servant of all" (Mark 9:35 NIV). Another time, James and John come to Jesus requesting positions of honor in the kingdom. Jesus reiterates the necessity of servant leadership in God's Kingdom. Even at the Last Supper the disciples continue to argue over who is greatest. Once more, Jesus explains: "the greatest among you should be like the youngest, and the one who rules like the one who serves. For who is greater, the one who is at the table or the one who serves? Is it not the one who is at the table? But I am among you as one who serves" (Luke 22:26-27 NIV).

The servant-leader is concerned primarily with meeting the needs of others. Perhaps the most graphic illustration of this style of leadership is found in the Fourth Servant Song in Isaiah 52:13-53:12. We discover a servant who is not only aware of the needs of humanity but becomes involved in their needs, sharing in their griefs and injuries. Verse 12, chapter 53 explains, "He poured out his life unto death, and was numbered with the transgressors. For he bore the sin of many, and made intercession for the transgressors" (NIV). The servant ministers by becoming involved on an equal level with those to whom he wishes to minister. He gives himself in order to meet the needs of others.

This principle of servant leadership is also present in the story of Esther. When a plot arises to destroy the Jews, Esther, a Jew who is married to the Persian king, has the option to remain silently comfortable in the security of her palace. Instead, she risks her life in order to save the lives of her people. Esther's choice to put the needs of others before her own results in a victory for the Jews over their enemies.

Early leaders in the church arose as people recognized how their gifts and abilities were able to meet needs. Stephen and six other men "full of the Spirit and wisdom" came to leadership positions to meet the needs of the widows of the Hellenized Christian community. Dorcas was a Christian leader in Joppa, where she "was always doing good and helping the poor." Lydia, the first convert in Philippi, opened her home to Paul and his companions on their missionary journey. Priscilla and Aquila assisted Paul while he was in Corinth and accompanied him to Ephesus where they taught Apollos "the way of God more accurately." In his letter to the church at Rome, Paul included a greeting to Priscilla and Aquila: "Greet Priscilla and Aquila, my fellow workers in Christ

Jesus. They risked their lives for me. Not only I but all the churches of the Gentiles are grateful to them."

Servant leadership exemplifies the biblical model for Christian leaders. Within this overall pattern, the Bible also speaks to numerous characteristics of leaders. While 1 Timothy 3:1-16 speaks specifically to the office of bishops and deacons, the traits listed here can have a broad general application to all leaders.

The writer begins with the mandate that leaders should not engage in misconduct. They should be blameless in their moral lives: temperate, prudent, respectable, gentle, and hospitable. They should be faithful to their families and able to exercise loving discipline in their homes. They should be spiritually mature people, not new converts, people who hold good standing within and without the faith community.

Also, 1 Peter 5:1-7 addresses issues of leadership. The author uses the image "shepherds of God's flock" to describe leaders—"serving as overseers—not because you must, but because you are willing, as God wants you to be; not greedy for money, but eager to serve; not lording it over those entrusted to you, but being examples to the flock" (vv. 2-3 NIV). Once again, Scripture echoes the theme of servant leadership.

What does a leader do?

As already noted, *a leader meets needs*. Throughout the Gospels, we see Jesus feeding the hungry and healing the sick. *A leader facilitates relationships*. Andrew brings his brother Peter to meet Jesus. Paul nurtures community in the churches he begins on his missionary journeys. *A leader also facilitates personal growth*. Again and again, Paul encourages Christians to grow in faith and obedience to God. *A leader models Christian living*. Paul is able to tell believers to imitate him as he imitates Christ because he himself has become a model for the gospel life.

A leader dreams, inspires, and supports. Nehemiah has a vision of a rebuilt wall of Jerusalem. He leads the people to return to the city and, against the odds, to rebuild the wall. *A leader takes courageous stands, often in the face of opposition*. Moses, despite his misgivings, stands before Pharaoh with God's message: "Let my people go." Shadrach, Meshach, and Abednego stand before Nebuchadnezzar, refusing to bow down to his statue.

A leader manages conflict. Often Jesus interrupts the bickering disciples. Paul pleads with Euodia and Syntyche to work out their differences. *A leader also shares leadership*. In Exodus 18, we see Jethro's wise counsel to Moses to divide leadership responsibilities with others. In the New Testament, Jesus calls out 12 men to share the work of his ministry. In Luke 10, He sends out 72 followers to proclaim His coming. Paul explains that we are co-laborers with God.

The central figure of Hermann Hesse's *Journey to the East* is Leo, the servant of a group of men on a journey. Leo performs menial chores for the group and sustains them with his spirit. The journey goes well until Leo disappears and the group falls apart. Without their servant, they are unable to continue their journey. Years later, one of the travelers finds Leo and is taken into the group which had sponsored the previous journey. He discovers that Leo is head of the group, its servant-leader.

God gifts individuals within the body of Christ with leadership qualities. The biblical model for the exercising of that gift is servant leadership, leadership symbolized more by a towel and a basin than a throne and a scepter. If God has called you as a leader, you have been invited to pattern yourself after Jesus himself, a leader who came not to be served but to serve.

From your perspective

1. Identify some characteristics of Jesus' model for leaders.

2. Review the book of Esther. How did she lead? What are some reasons you would have assumed Esther was not a natural leader?

3. What is the strongest characteristic, in your opinion, which revealed Esther's true "leader nature"?

Uniquely gifted for servant leadership

Susan Shaw

♡

Following the will of God and doing His work is the task of every believer. Over and over again, the Bible witnesses to the leadership and ministry roles of women. Perhaps the most compelling biblical basis for women in leadership is an understanding of the freedom of God's Spirit to bestow gifts upon women and men. All Christians are part of the body of Christ, and each part of the body has a function to fulfill. Paul reminds us in Galatians 3:28, "There is neither Jew nor Greek, slave nor free, male nor female, for you are all one in Christ Jesus" (NIV).

God has given each one of us gifts for building up the body of Christ. We are responsible for nurturing those gifts and exercising them in the world. Women, as well as men, may have the gift of leadership. Nowhere does Scripture lead us to believe that the gifts are in some way gender related. If God has gifted you with leadership, then your responsibility to God and to the Body, the Church, is to lead.

The Bible has provided us with multitudes of models to follow— Eunice, Lois, Lydia, Priscilla, Deborah, Esther, Mary, Martha, Dorcas, and Anna. But the most appropriate model of all is Jesus. Drawing on His understanding of God's nature, Jesus develops a style of servant leadership, balancing His call to action on the part of the gospel with His own nurturing love of His followers.

This is the kind of leader God calls Christian leaders to be. Christian leaders are to stand against sin and for right. They are to persuade others to live the gospel life. They are to challenge people to deeper commitment to Christ. But they are always to do this through servanthood.

Women can bring their inherent nurturing gifts and concerns for relationships to servant leadership. In Genesis 2:18,20, woman is described as man's helper. This word is never used in Scripture to designate a subordinate. In fact, it is used to refer to God who is our helper (Psalm 146:5). The calling to servant leadership is a high calling for it is a calling to follow in the steps of Christ who became a servant.

Many biblical images depict God's nurturing activity through experiences common to women. Isaiah 49:15 shows God sustaining people like a nursing mother: "Can a mother forget the baby at her breast and have no compassion on the child she has borne? Though she may forget, I will not forget you!" (NIV).

In Numbers 11:11-12, we find Moses complaining to God about the weight of His responsibility as leader of the Hebrew people: "What have I done to displease you that you put the burden of all these people on me? Did I conceive all these people? Did I give them birth? Why do you tell me to carry them in my arms, as a nurse carries an infant, to the land you promised on oath to their forefathers?" (NIV). Moses is saying to God, since you're the one who conceived them and gave them birth, you ought to be the one to nurse them. God hears Moses' complaint and provides assistance for Moses.

Other images show God's childcare as God takes care of people in ways traditionally ascribed to women. Isaiah 46:3 depicts God as carrying children: "You whom I have upheld since you were conceived, and have carried since your birth" (NIV). Isaiah 66:13 pictures God comforting a child: "As a mother comforts her child, so will I comfort you" (NIV). In Hosea 11:3-4 we see God teaching the people of Israel to walk: "It was I who taught Ephraim to walk, taking them by the arms; I led them with cords of human kindness, with ties of love; I lifted the yoke from their neck and bent down to feed them" (NIV). Matthew 6:28-30 show God as clothing people: "If that is how God clothes the grass of the field, which is here today and tomorrow is thrown into the fire, will he not much more clothe you?" (v. 30 NIV).

In these images, we see God nurturing people as a parent nurtures children. Women need to bring their unique gifts to ministry and leadership because these gifts provide a balance to ministry—a balance of mothering and fathering which is rooted in God's care for us.

Psychologist Carol Gilligan sees adult maturity as a balance between rights and responsibilities. Her work demonstrates that men tend to approach the world from a standpoint of detachment, with concern for justice and fairness. Women tend to approach the world from a standpoint of attachment, with concern for care and relationships. In the Bible, we find Jesus as the model for the balance between rights and relationships. In the Sermon on the Mount, Jesus modifies the old law with its stringent system of justice in light of His new ethic of love. When questioned about His sabbath practices, Jesus responds that the sabbath was made for people and not people for the sabbath. Jesus balances law with love. For Jesus, justice occurs in the context of relationship. Jesus transcends the "eye for an eye" of the Old Testament law and opts for including one's enemies in the list of one's love relationships.

Jesus Himself demonstrates this kind of nurturing love which does good to those who hate. In Matthew 23:37, Jesus laments, "O Jerusalem, Jerusalem, you who kill the prophets and stone those sent to you, how often I have longed to gather your children together, as a hen gathers her chicks under her wings, but you were not willing" (NIV). Jesus uses the mother hen image to picture the nurture and protection God offers.

The Old Testament is also full of images of finding shelter under God's wings. Psalm 17:9 requests, "Keep me as the apple of your eye; hide me in the shadow of your wings" (NIV). Psalm 61:4 states, "I long to dwell in your tent forever and take refuge in the shelter of your wings" (NIV).

Jesus values the nurturing gifts which women bring to leadership and ministry. He even sees Himself as a nurturer to His people. And because of His familiarity with Scripture, Jesus, too, would have known the Bible's own affirmation of God's nurturing activities. We see Jesus echoing this affirmation of women's special gifts for ministry in the way He treats women.

From early in the ministry of Jesus, women are among the most faithful disciples. Luke 8:1-3 tells us, "Jesus traveled about from one town and village to another, proclaiming the good news of the Kingdom of God. The Twelve were with Him, and also some women who had been cured of evil spirits and diseases: Mary (called Magdalene) from whom seven demons had come out; Joanna the wife of Cuza, the manager of Herod's household; Susanna; and many others. These women were helping to support them out of their own means" (NIV).

Church historian Jeremias calls this "an unprecedented happening in the history of that time . . . . Jesus knowingly overthrew custom when He allowed women to follow Him . . . . Jesus was not content with bringing women up on a higher plane than was the custom; but as Saviour of all, He brings them before God on an equal footing with men."

In John 4:1-42, we find the remarkable story of Jesus and the woman at the well. Of the many astonishing elements of this story, perhaps the most notable is that Jesus discusses theology with a woman in public. In the Jewish world of Jesus' day, a man did not speak to a woman in public, not even his own wife. Even more unlikely was a rabbi's discussing theology with a woman. Yet Jesus offers salvation to this woman who, in turn, brings many Samaritans to faith.

Two women with whom Jesus has a close relationship are the sisters Mary and Martha. Luke 10:38-42 relates the story of tension between Mary and Martha over roles. Mary sits at the feet of Jesus listening to His teaching while Martha prepares the meal. Mary's position hardly fits a woman's role in Jesus' day. She puts herself in the position of a disciple; yet in that time, women were not allowed to touch the Scriptures, nor were they taught the Torah by a rabbi.

Jesus commends Mary's choice. He says, "Mary has chosen what is better." He affirms Mary's personhood and her right to decide her way of following Him. John identifies Mary as ministering to Jesus when she anoints Him with expensive perfume (John 12:1-3). Again, Jesus defends Mary's right to exercise her understanding of her ministry.

The Bible is full of other examples of women who lead out in ministering, exercising their gifts in order to build up Christ's body. These women are role models for women today whom God has gifted for servant leadership in their churches.

In 2 Timothy 1:5 we read of the faith of Eunice and Lois which has been handed on to Timothy. Luke 2:36-38 relates the story of the prophetess Anna's witness about Jesus. Anna, the devout widow who spends time in the temple fasting and praying, confirms Jesus "to all who were looking forward to the redemption of Jerusalem" (v. 38 NIV).

Women are the first to carry the good news of the resurrection. Matthew 28:8-10 tells us, "So the women hurried away from the tomb, afraid yet filled with joy, and ran to tell his disciples. Suddenly Jesus met them. 'Greetings,' he said. They came to Him, clasped His feet, and worshiped Him. Then Jesus said to them, 'Do not be afraid. Go and tell my brothers to go to Galilee; there they will see me'" (NIV).

The book of Acts begins with Peter's sermon on the day of Pentecost in which he quotes from the prophet Joel: "In the last days, God says,

I will pour out my Spirit on all people. Your sons and daughters will prophesy, your young men will see visions, your old men will dream dreams. Even on my servants, both men and women, I will pour out my Spirit in those days, and they will prophesy" (Acts 2:17-18 NIV).

One prominent woman in the book of Acts is Priscilla. Acts 18:24-26 tells us that Priscilla instructed Apollos, a gifted preacher, in "the way of God more adequately." Lydia (Acts 16:11-15) is an important factor in the development of the Philippian church. Acts 21:9 tells us of Philip's four daughters who prophesy. The purpose of prophesy is to convict those outside God's will and to call people to be accountable to God. In 1 Corinthians 14:34 we read that prophesy also has value in the edification, exhortation, and comfort of the believers.

In Romans 16:1-2, Paul greets Phoebe, a deaconess of the church at Cenchreae. Paul commends her as "a great help to many people, including me." In verse 7 of that chapter, Paul writes, "Greet Andronicus and Junias, my relatives who have been in prison with me. They are outstanding among the apostles, and they were in Christ before I was." In the Greek, the name used is Junian which may be masculine or feminine. Chrysostom, writing in the first century, assumed Junian to be a woman. He exclaims, "Oh! how great is the devotion of this woman, that she should be even counted worthy of the appelation apostle."

In the Old Testament, a number of women exercise the prophetic gift. Exodus 15:20 refers to Miriam as a prophetess. In Judges 4, we find the story of Deborah, a prophetess, who "was leading Israel at that time" (v. 4 NIV). Second Kings 22:14 mentions Huldah who is a prophetess. Another Old Testament role model for women is found in Naomi. Ruth has seen faithfulness to God, and as Naomi begins her return to her people, Ruth makes this vow: "Where you go I will go, and where you stay I will stay. Your people will be my people and your God my God" (Ruth 1:16 NIV). Through Naomi's witness, Ruth comes to embrace the God of the Hebrews.

As I think back over my own faith pilgrimage, I remember the many women who by their own lives of faith nurtured me in mine—Sunday School teachers, Girls in Action leaders, camp counselors. These were women who had responded to God's call to be ministering servant-leaders. They brought their individual gifts to ministry, gifts rooted in the very nature of God.

From your perspective

1. Have you been introduced to some leaders with whom you were not familiar? Who were they?

2. What were some of the gifts they utilized in their lives?

3. Identify some of the gifts God has given you. Are you utilizing your gifts in your leadership role?

What am I doing leading this parade? I didn't even plan to march!

Beverly Sutton

If you've been in church (or almost any other organized group) for very long, you probably know the feeling. You suggest something that is needed, a ministry or project, an improvement for a current activity. Before you know it, you have been pressed, nudged, or shoved into leadership of the very project you suggested. Better yet, your group elects officers at the meeting you miss during a family vacation. At the next meeting, you're greeted with, "We prayed about it, and we all thought you would be such a good president. We need a change, and you always have such good ideas. We knew you wouldn't mind if we elected you, and we'll do all we can to help."

Whatever route you may have traveled, chances are great that you have held a position of formal or informal leadership sometime during your Christian experience. Do you see yourself as a leader? Or do you quickly push aside such ideas with comments like, "I'm not really a leader. I'm just doing this job until they find someone else"?

When you think of a leader, whose portrait do you see framed in your mental picture? From your experience as both leader and follower, how would you define or describe leadership? Some descriptive ideas about leaders and leadership are included in the answers to questions on this short test. Compare your conclusions with ours.

Leadership: A true/false test

_____ 1. Leadership requires a specialized spiritual gift.
_____ 2. All leaders have followers.
_____ 3. Leaders are born, not made.
_____ 4. Women are better leaders than men.
_____ 5. Every Christian woman is a leader.
_____ 6. The leader of the group is always the person in front.
_____ 7. Leadership involves change.
_____ 8. Leaders are risk takers.
_____ 9. To be a good leader, a person needs a strong, forceful personality.
_____ 10. Leaders are people who can do the work better than the followers.
_____ 11. Leaders must have vision.
_____ 12. Good leaders look alike.

1. Leadership requires a specialized spiritual gift. FALSE
While both Romans 12 and 1 Corinthians 12 tell us that God chooses to give some people the gift of administration or leadership, both Scripture references imply that all the spiritual gifts involve leadership. Because of her gifts, each person leads differently and at different times, but each *does* lead.

Leadership, then, is not a rare skill or a mantle placed on the shoulders of a privileged few. Instead, it is a function of our spiritual gifts and our calling to equip us to do our part to share God's good news and strengthen other believers. The verb *lead* is defined as "moving to show the way or direct the course of, by going before or along with." Add this further explanation, "to guide, to cause to follow." Among these definitions is an approach to leadership to complement each of the spiritual gifts.

2. All leaders have followers. TRUE
Talitha, a high school senior looking elegant and innocent in her white eyelet, floor-length formal had led one of six columns of 50 flag bearers to the platform at the civic center. We were rehearsing the ceremony in which flags of nations and states to which Southern Baptists send missionaries were presented. As the music began for the flag parade to leave the platform, Talitha continued to stand at the front of the column looking composed and beautiful, every bit the leader. Unfortunately she failed to hear the musical cue for her column to leave. The flagbearers, recognizing the error, simply reversed their

24

direction and left the platform. Minutes later, Talitha turned to see the last flagbearers leaving the room. Panicked, she gathered her long skirt in her arms revealing the dirty tennis shoes she had chosen to wear with her formal. She jumped off the platform and ran down the aisle toward the receding flag column shouting, "Wait for me. I'm your leader." In a flash Talitha understood the truth of the axiom, "If you're leading, but no one is following, you're just taking a walk." Whether leading the parade, serving as president, organizing the family, or guiding one other person, a leader must lead at least one follower.

3. Leaders are born, not made. FALSE

For those of us who are reluctant leaders, it would be easier to believe that some people are just born leaders and others are created to follow. A more responsible approach to leadership asserts that every Christian is a priest accountable to God for the use of his or her gifts and opportunities. This view, mentioned in the answer to question number one, includes the idea that every Christian can develop strong leadership skills to make the best use of his or her gifts and opportunities. Of course, some of us will be better—or at least more charismatic— leaders than others, but everyone must learn to accept leadership roles. If leaders are made rather than born, then it is both possible and appropriate to be the leader of the hour rather than of a lifetime. It also makes it easier for leaders and followers to reverse roles according to the needs of the hour. For instance, Sarah, a school principal, and her secretary Alicia attend the same church. At church, Alicia serves as Sarah's Sunday School teacher.

4. Women are better leaders than men. FALSE

Surprised? Were you expecting the question stated in reverse order or an argument for feminist approaches to leadership? It's a fact; women are no better than men as leaders. They are no worse than men as leaders, either! The major differences in leadership between men and women relate to style rather than substance.

The commentator on a local radio call-in show posed the question, "Should a woman be elected president of the United States?" After several callers questioned whether women could be hard, forceful, and decisive enough to be powerful and effective presidents, a caller suggested that Margaret Thatcher, then British Prime Minister, exhibited all these leadership characteristics. Promptly, another caller replied, "Mrs. Thatcher doesn't really count as a female leader. She's more like a man with a handbag and gloves." His point: real women don't exhibit public power.

As major corporations adopt success formulas for the 1990s, many are beginning to seek new styles of executive leadership. They are replacing authoritarian power approaches emphasizing only the final results with more sensitive, people-oriented approaches emphasizing the process as well as the goal. In short, organizations that have required women in leadership to adopt male leadership styles are beginning recognize the strengths of feminine approaches to leadership.

What about church? The case for feminine approaches to leadership is even stronger here. The servant leadership taught and modeled by Jesus includes many of the characteristics we label as feminine: teaching; modeling; communicating; caring; nurturing; networking.

In business, home, and church, both women and men serve effectively as leaders. Often they lead their followers to the same destination, but they leave different footprints along the way.

5. Every Christian woman is a leader. TRUE

Are you thinking, "That can't be true; because I'm a Christian, and I'm not a leader. Besides, if we are all leaders, who is going to follow?" Christians who share two basic beliefs recognize the responsibility of every believer, male or female, to be a leader.

If, as discussed earlier, every Christian has at least one spiritual gift to use to strengthen the body of believers, every Christian is responsible for leading others through the use of that gift. Add to this the doctrine which has energized Christian congregations since the time of Jesus, the priesthood of every believer. Based on Exodus 19:5-6, 1 Peter 1:1-10, and numerous other Scriptures, this doctrine suggests that each of us is accountable to God for at least three actions: leading lost people to Christ; ministering to people who have spiritual, emotional, or physical needs; and growing in Christian discipleship.

A better way to write the sentence in the test would be "Every Christian woman who is growing in discipleship is a leader." She may be called to manage large groups or to lead one person at a time, but her call to leadership is clear.

6. The leader of the group is always the person in front. FALSE

Was this statement too obvious? A friend who read this laughingly suggested as an illustration a row of ducklings swimming along behind their mother. The duckling in the middle of the row is wearing a baseball cap bearing the words, "I'm the leader!" Comical? Certainly. Possible? Absolutely.

Although many secular leadership books make a case for leaders to be the ones, "out front," personal experience teaches us differently—at least on the surface. Have you ever taken a leadership position because of the encouragement and guidance of someone in the group whom you admire or respect? Has your church ever called an inexperienced staff member who had great potential; then, one or two nurturing individuals adopted him and nudged him forward as a leader? One of the strongest kinds of leaders is the cool-headed, affirming encourager. This leader, like a duckling in the middle of the row, doesn't swim at the head of the parade, but leads by carrying the compass, giving advanced swimming lessons, or helping the lead swimmer avoid the rapids.

7. Leadership involves change. TRUE

This may be the toughest aspect of leadership. While all of us recognize that change is essential to life, few of us enjoy change that we don't initiate. Nevertheless, leadership, like discipleship, requires moving forward. This, of course, means changing and leading others to accept or initiate positive changes.

Have you ever belonged to an organization which routinely elected a president or director but didn't allow her to lead it to do anything new, or perhaps anything at all? Obviously, people who are standing still do not need a leader. No matter what they call her, she serves only as coordinator or moderator—someone who simply observes the current situation and interests of the group and organizes to help them perpetuate it comfortably.

Groups, causes, or organizations which do not encourage and plan for positive change quickly die. Occasionally they are destroyed by external forces. More often, though, they wither within. The structure or shell may remain, but the heartbeat is gone.

8. Leaders are risk takers. TRUE

There is more to risk taking than skydiving and auto racing. All leaders risk, but not all who risk are leaders. Some people risk for the thrill of living on the edge. Leaders risk to help followers achieve their goal.

Remember the parable of the talents in Matthew 25? The master gave three servants varying amounts of money to use while he was away. When he returned, he rewarded the two who had invested their money and doubled it, but he condemned the one who buried his. This parable, like hundreds of other Scriptures throughout the Bible, illustrates the command for all Christians to take risks responsibly.

Responsible risking may be the most invigorating and maturing aspect of Christian leadership. Dr. Keith Parks, president of the Southern Baptist Foreign Mission Board, challenged new missionary appointees by saying, "God has called you to go around the world for the most exciting and basic purpose given to Christians. He has not promised ease or visible results. Instead, he may ask you to risk comfort, convenience, family, even your life for the sake of his message."

Not all risks carry the same price tags. There may be more subtle risks of investing in the life of an unlikely follower or putting your reputation on the line for the sake of a cause or an individual.

A Christian leader should answer questions like these to decide whether a risk is appropriate:

•Will this action help accomplish the goal?

•Is the action compatible with the mission and values of the group?

•Is the action in the best interest of the group?

•Are the goals and possible outcome worth the risk?

•What will happen if I (we) do not do this?

•Are there other actions I (we) can take which accomplish the goal with less risk?

•When possible, did those who may have to pay the consequences of the action have a part in the decision?

9. A good leader needs a strong, forceful personality. FALSE

As you read the stories of leaders in chapter one, you probably recognized some who are much like leaders you know. The differences in leadership style among these leaders are obvious.

Many good leaders depend on strength and power of personality to persuade people to adopt their goal or vision. Others find their strengths in organizing, amassing large amounts of information about specific subjects, developing detailed processes to achieve the goal, or displaying competency in other ways. Warmth, loyalty, quiet influence, affirmation, and creation of a sense of security and belonging in the group may be the preferred style of other leaders. Still others inspire followship through the strength of their ideals and high expectations for themselves and others.

All of these styles are valid approaches to leadership. Think of the leaders—formal and informal—who have influenced you. Which approaches were most natural for them? How would you describe your own style?

10. Leaders can do the work better than followers. FALSE

If you are employed or work as a volunteer in a business or other large organization, you probably know leaders who do not have the same specialized skills as some of their employees. On the other hand, you may know people who can perform the most amazing, intricate tasks but cannot explain a task to others or inspire them to attempt it.

While a leader may not be able to do the job better than her followers, she equips and inspires them to do the job better than she. Often, the mark of a good leader is her ability to surround herself with skilled people whom she enables to achieve the goal.

11. Leaders must have vision. TRUE

What separates the real leader from the moderator, manager, coordinator, or the person who merely occupies the leadership chair? Vision! The leader has a clear picture of a better way things could be. Having vision, though, doesn't necessarily mean a person is a leader. A visionary dreams or imagines the ultimate goal, but a leader combines the dream with the actions necessary to make it happen. God may have given your organization the vision to change your community by teaching adult nonreaders to read, helping unemployed people to find jobs, or providing after-school activities for latchkey kids. Through these you will share Christ with the community. Another example of vision is the church that adopts a nation or group of people with little or no Christian influence and prays daily for that group until a strong missions base is established there.

Think of a group to which you belong. A clear sense of vision can do several things. It magnifies the group's purpose. Vision clarifies the direction the group should be taking, allowing you to decide both what you will and you will not do. Vision focuses attention on purpose rather than structure and helps the group avoid petty arguments and unimportant activities. It gives members courage to take a stand and enthusiasm to act. Vision builds fellowship and attracts new members with the same interests. Finally, vision leads your group to climb out of the pit of empty tradition, resistance to change, and complacency.

As a leader, how can you know your dream for the people you lead is the vision God has for them? How do you get people to buy into the vision? There is no simple formula, but these guidelines may help:
(A) As you begin to have a strong mental picture of the positive outcome your group can achieve, test the dream with questions like these:
- Have I spent enough time with God in prayer and Bible study to see the work of the Holy Spirit in this?
- Does this vision fit the mission and values of the group?
- Is the vision challenging, but possible to accomplish?
- Have I gathered the necessary information to make this decision?
- Am I willing to see this through to the finish?
- Is the outcome worth the cost?

29

(B) Share your vision with two or three leaders or dreamers in the group. Discuss the vision, listening to their concerns and ideas. Give them time to buy into the vision.

(C) Try to write the vision in a few sentences. Is the description simple, specific, challenging, and focused on your purpose? Does it emphasize both people and God's power at work in your group? Make necessary changes.

(D) Share the vision with the group you lead. Expect resistance. Be positive, giving attention to both spoken and unspoken concerns.

(E) Work to get people to accept the vision as a direction both for the group and for themselves personally. Take time to include as many as possible in the dream. Often the larger group will not catch the whole vision until they can see the first concrete results.

(F) Take action. Many visions are stifled while waiting for unanimous consent or all conflict to be resolved. Remember, though, that the price for achieving the vision may be high.

(G) Keep sharing the vision in as many ways as possible until the group claims it as their own.

12. Good leaders look alike. TRUE

Imagine a large billboard on the side of the highway. Featured on the billboard are leaders who have influenced you positively. They may be Sunday School teachers, missions leaders, employers, coaches, teachers, club officers, relatives, or pastors. They are standing in a row, larger than life and in living color. Does your mental lineup include an array of characters—short, tall, curly-haired, bald, male, female, shy, bold, enthusiastic, and serious? On the surface they look quite different, and their leadership styles and situations vary widely. Nevertheless, good leaders do look or act alike in several ways. Some common characteristics have been mentioned in the answers to the test questions in this chapter. Others can be summarized in three focus areas.

Focus on people

Effective leaders focus on people first. Although leadership involves moving toward a goal, leaders help people accomplish the task. For each of the leadership actions listed here, try placing the names of leaders on your billboard in the blank. Are these actions characteristic?

1._____ helps others function independently and cooperatively. To do this, the leader takes time to recognize needs, abilities, and attitudes of individual followers as well as strengths of the group.

2._____ communicates. She takes time to share her vision, the steps to accomplish the task, information about the task, her concern for others, and dozens of other messages to strengthen the group.

Effective leaders suggest these steps to productive communication:

(A) Ask questions to determine the spoken or unspoken message.

(B) Listen creatively to hear the spoken and unspoken response.

(C) Share the message clearly and positively.

(D) Listen to the response of the other.

(E) Check to be sure that both of you understand the message.

3._____ delegates responsibilities. For any good leader, delegation is a must, both to accomplish the task and to develop the skills and confidence of followers. It is time to delegate when you aren't getting the job done, when you are spending time on little things that others could do, when some in the group have much more to do than others. Delegate when a job requires specialized skills, others need or want a challenge, or followers need to buy into the project.

The leader who delegates responsibilities well chooses someone who understands and shares her vision for the project. She explains the job to be accomplished including standards, deadlines, and limitations. She gives the person the authority needed to complete the project, including budget and resources. Then, she lets go of the project! Finally, she provides support and expects success.

4._____ manages conflict positively. Conflict is an almost inevitable element of change and risk-taking leadership. It can either set back progress or lead to growth. My first lesson in conflict management came when my mother used a switch from the peach tree to settle a sibling conflict at our house. This example was followed by the elementary school principal who made boys caught fighting on the playground don boxing gloves, step into the ring, and slug it out. Positive conflict management starts where these examples did, with the leader facing the problem realistically, honestly, and as directly as possible within the limitations of the situation. An important second step is to understand not only the words spoken but the underlying messages. A good leader respects resistance as an opportunity for re-evaluating approaches to the task as well as clarifying the vision.

Next, the leader looks for creative alternatives to meet the needs of as many as possible and implements the best solution. She demonstrates the same positive regard for all those involved in the conflict.

31

5._____ models the way. Was it easier to put a name in this blank than in the others? Many of us remember best the leaders who have led by example. Although personally demanding, practicing what we preach often makes the best argument for the stand we take or the cause we promote. Modeling also helps the leader build and develop the self esteem of others. Through modeling the way to accomplish the task, the leader can instruct followers, recognize and affirm gifts and abilities, and encourage others to catch her vision.

Focus on tasks

Effective leaders balance their emphasis on people with a strong commitment to the task. In fact, some define leadership as the ability to get a job done through others. Just as you identified the people strengths of outstanding leaders you know, now test their task-related characteristics. Put their names in the blanks in this list of task actions.

1._____ demonstrates an unswerving commitment to the task or cause. All of us know people who are so identified with a cause that their names come to mind immediately in connection with that subject. We may even say things like "Mrs. Turner is Miss Missions around here," or "Brother Greg is leading us to be known as the church that prays for people." Although not every illustration is so obvious, the combination of well-defined vision and obvious commitment to achieve the task are essential for the leader to attract followers and challenge them to act.

2._____ sets challenging, but reachable, goals. The secret to confidence in leadership is the ability to set a clear, challenging, attainable goal and intermediate goals to reach it. Once goals are set and communicated, the leader and followers know where to begin and what to expect. Goal-setting helps the leader clarify her mission so that the group can buy into it. It enables followers to recognize how they can contribute to the cause. It allows the leader to simplify the workload by avoiding unnecessary activities and concentrating on productive ones. Finally, goal-setting provides common ground for leader and followers to recognize progress and make course corrections.

3._____ takes initiative. Throughout the Bible, God urges leaders who follow Him to take initiatives acting out their faith in His power and guidance. Few illustrations are more dramatic than the incident recorded in Exodus 14:13-15 when the Israelites, chased by the Egyptian army, are cowering on the bank of the Red Sea. Moses encouraged his frantic followers with more certainty than he really felt. Apparently, he began praying earnestly for God's deliverance. God answered by telling him to quit his crying out and take the initiative to raise his rod and send his people across on dry land.

Every effective leader faces the moment when prayer and preparation culminate in taking the risk to initiate action. Making difficult decisions and accepting responsibility for them is at the core of effective leadership.

4._____ excels in tough situations. In an ongoing argument about the merits of a recent United States president, a friend said, "Oh sure, he's a nice guy and a great leader—during the good times." His argument, of course, is that the strength of a leader is not known until it is tested by adversity. Moses' situation described in the previous question is an example of extreme adversity as he stood between a disgruntled and frightened rabble of followers and the Red Sea. It is difficult to know whether he felt more endangered by the approaching Egyptians or his own followers. There is little question, though, about the strength of his leadership.

In tough situations, vision and commitment to the cause bring strength and the leadership qualities of persistence and courage surface.

Most of the difficult situations we face as leaders are more subtle and less spectacular than Moses'. Instead, they may relate to internal conflict in the group, taking an unpopular stand, or economic difficulties. Whatever the setting, strong leaders emerge in tough times.

5._____ fails successfully. While it sounds incongruous, a vital element of leadership is the ability to recognize and accept failure and to move past it positively. Effective leaders view failure as an element of progress, not a criticism or condemnation of their leadership or vision. A good leader does not let failure discourage followers but affirms their willingness to try, acknowledges their progress, and directs them toward the next step to accomplish the goal.

Focus on servanthood

Many secular leaders excel in focusing on people and tasks. The strength of Christian leaders, only poorly imitated by secular leaders, is found in modeling leadership after Jesus, the ultimate servant-leader. The Christian leader, empowered by the Holy Spirit, views her role from an entirely different frame of reference than her secular counterpart. She is uniquely equipped as a servant to use her leadership power to meet the needs of followers as an act of service to her master.

These characteristics of a servant, discussed by Charles R. Swindoll in his book *Improving Your Serve*, summarize the ways servant leaders look alike. The servant leader, says Swindoll, is a person who demonstrates transparent humanity, genuine humility, absolute honesty, and proper perspective for life.

A final word

Dr. Ida V. Moffatt, the pioneer nurse educator who founded the school of nursing at Samford University, excels as a Christian leader. She shares these practical principles which have molded her approach to leadership.

- •Allow yourself to care.
- •Do not exploit people with organization and methodology.
- •Do not limit people's freedom and decision making.
- •Do not set up organizational patterns that are barriers to direct communication.
- •Be willing to transfer some comfort and convenience to others.
- •Work hard to build self confidence in others.

The next time you find yourself at the head of the parade, whether in a leadership position you eagerly sought or grudgingly accepted, take some time to answer the 12 questions discussed here. Then lead on.

From your perspective

1. How did you arrive in the leadership role you now have (officer, chairperson, teacher, leader, etc.) ?

2. What did you discern regarding your personal perspective of leadership from the true/false exercise?

3. What steps can you take to enhance your leadership role? When will you do this? How do you see this changing your "leader look"?

Who is that leader in the mirror?
Barbara Curnutt

♡

Pick up the nearest magazine with a colorful picture on the cover. Look at the picture for a moment, then turn the magazine over and see what you remember. List every descriptive detail you can recall from the picture.

This simple activity illustrates the fact that we are constantly taking mental and emotional pictures of events, objects, and people around us. We are creating mental and emotional images. An image is a portrait, representation, or idea. Our self-image is our picture; it is the way we project ourselves. It is also the way others perceive us.

Even an organization has an image. Often that image is projected through personalities who lead or comprise the group. Think about the perceived images of organizations in which you are involved. Do they reflect the personalities of those who lead?

Image is a powerful force. And the image others have of us as leaders is photographed in three basic ways:
•the way we perceive ourselves;
•the way we present ourselves;
•the way we perform our task.

The way we perceive ourselves
Give yourself a self-esteem check. Take an honest look at your life

and list specific things you like about yourself. If you could change anything about yourself, what would you change? The questions may seem elementary, but the way we perceive ourselves greatly colors the way others perceive us, as well as the way we perceive others. According to pastor and author Calvin Miller, "However high your own self-esteem rises, you do see other people. You observe them and measure all that they are against all that you are."

What is self-esteem? In *The Antecedents of Self-Esteem*, Stanley Coopersmith defines self-esteem as "the evaluation which the individual makes and customarily maintains with regard to himself: it expresses an attitude of approval or disapproval, and indicates the extent to which the individual believes himself to be capable, significant, successful, and worthy."

Do you see yourself as capable and significant, uniquely created in God's image? At the same time, are you willing to acknowledge your blind spots when lovingly confronted? The ability to take an open, honest look at oneself is an essential part of becoming a leader.

In Paul's letter to the Roman church, Scripture affirms the importance of self-evaluation. "For by the grace given me I say to every one of you: Do not think of yourself more highly than you ought, but rather think of yourself with sober judgment, in accordance with the measure of faith God has given you" (Rom. 12:3 NIV).

Think about your own gifts, talents, special skills, and personality traits. What qualities do you bring to your leadership position? Now think about areas of weakness. As a leader, what would you identify as your limitations?

To think that no two persons have been created exactly alike is both humbling and empowering. The fact that each of us is a unique creation in identity and expression reassures us of God's infinite, intimate love. Read Psalm 139 and celebrate your Creator.

All of us experience feelings of insecurity and inadequacy from time to time. It is normal that we do. It serves as a good reminder that we are nothing apart from the power of Christ at work within us. For in our weakness, God's power is made perfect. However, to live life in bondage to poor self-esteem is not God's intention.

When we feel good about ourselves, we face life with confidence, strength, and honesty. Because our self-worth is not dependent on the approval of others, we are able to give and receive unconditional love. We are even free to risk failure.

However, if we do not like ourselves, we tend to devalue and punish ourselves. Rather than meeting life with confidence, we react out of fear, intimidation, and defeat. In our struggle to find security, we allow everyone else to make our decisions and control our emotions. In other words, we live life as people-pleasers.

A person who does not value herself will constantly expect someone else to provide that value. Sadly, those unrealistic expectations of others usually result in unfair demands and manipulations, often alienating her from those she seeks to please.

As long as we are in search of self-worth through external gratification, our lives will be controlled by the whims and wishes of others rather than the Spirit of God. Before long, we will find ourselves resenting others for pressuring us into molds of their own design.

Some of us have the idea that our worth is related to how much we do. We live in a very production-oriented society. More often than not, success is measured by productivity. We need to remember that we can never do enough to earn our self-esteem. Our self-worth must be rooted in something more than a position, profession, or possessions.

When our self-esteem becomes rooted in God-esteem, we will no longer need to compare ourselves to everyone else. Our frantic search for others' approval will cease. We can celebrate our own uniqueness and all that we possess as joint-heirs with Christ.

"The Spirit himself testifies with our spirit that we are God's children. Now if we are children, then we are heirs—heirs of God and co-heirs with Christ" (Rom. 8:16-17a NIV).

There was never any question who Jesus sought to please. He is our supreme example of single-minded devotion to God. Living in complete dependence on God freed Jesus to be all that He was called to be, in spite of the pressures and demands of others.

When our lives are lived in total dependence on God, we will experience the peace and serenity that Christ's presence provides. We will be comfortable with ourselves. As leaders, we will be content with our judgments and decisions. Neither crises, conflicts, nor criticisms will defeat us when our mind is stayed on Him.

Leaders who have had the greatest impact in history possessed this quality of single-mindedness. Consider other role models from Scripture who were inner directed, such as Abraham, Joseph, and Nehemiah. Each of these men faced uncertainties following God's call and could have been distracted, discouraged, even defeated if not for their singleness of purpose.

The Apostle Paul could have been sidetracked with any number of issues facing the early church and yet he said, "This one thing I do ."

The more we grow in fellowship with the Father, the more focused and purposeful we will become. There is no substitute for maintaining an inner-directed life apart from alone time with God. It is in aloneness and quietness that the character of leadership is formed.

The way we present ourselves

Our image is projected in many ways, but more often than not it is shaped by the way we present ourselves. We may possess a strong, positive self-image, yet fail to project ourselves publicly in a positive light.

Because we never get a second chance to make a first impression, physical appearance becomes important. This is not to imply that one has to be a gorgeous, 20-year-old model to be effective. Many effective leaders would not be described as young and beautiful, yet, our appearance influences the way others perceive us as leaders.

Reflect on Paul's admonition to the Corinthians: "Don't you know that you yourselves are God's temple and that God's Spirit lives in you?"(1 Cor. 3:16 NIV) "Do you not know that your body is a temple of the Holy Spirit, who is in you, whom you have received from God? You are not your own; you were bought at a price. Therefore honor God with your body" (1 Cor. 6:19-20 NIV).

Once we grasp the fact that God indwells us, it should affect how we view and treat our bodies. If we are temples of the Holy Spirit, then it should matter how we present ourselves. Recognizing that we are created in God's image, we should be conscious of our appearance, yet we should seek to maintain a spirit of humility. It is one thing to be sensitive; it is altogether different to be consumed with appearance.

In light of the passage we have just read, exercise should be a priority for all Christians. Exercise enhances mental ability, overall health, and perspective on life. Consistent exercise definately helps relieve stress and maintain weight control. Why would you not want to exercise if the results are so beneficial?

Let's look now at specific areas that affect our appearance. Although it is our least favorite subject, weight is the most obvious place to begin. When was the last time you made an objective evaluation? Whether for health reasons or for appearance sake, begin now to work to remove those unnecessary pounds.

What about your hair? Do you have a good cut that complements your face? How about your nails? Are they neatly trimmed? Is your makeup appropriate, not over done?

Clothing is another key area that affects our image. The issue here is not quantity or expense. Too many of us cram and stuff our closets and drawers with things we seldom wear. The important thing is that your wardrobe is suited to your shape, size, and skin color. Be conscious of coordinating colors and clothing pieces. If you need help, ask the advice of a friend whose taste in clothing you appreciate. Maintain a sharp wardrobe by eliminating the unnecessary and concentrating on a few right outfits. Keep it simple; avoid the gaudy or flashy. Remember you do not need a closet full of clothes or a purse full of cash to present a positive image.

The idea is simply to be conscious of the public image you are projecting. Be sensitive to what is appropriate. For example, there may be instances when pants, jeans, or shorts might be unacceptable for you as a leader. Be yourself, but be wise.

While physical appearance is vital to our self-image, there are other ways in which we present ourselves. Some of those ways are communicated verbally, others non-verbally. Both are equally important.

Ask yourself: When I enter a room, does my presence say "Here I am!" or "There you are!"? Is it necessary for you to be the center of attention or are you comfortable allowing the focus to be on others?

Personalities are translated through communication. When you talk, all of you talks. Not only do you communicate verbally, but through facial expressions, body positions and voice tone as well.

Because communication is multifaceted, words can say one thing while the body, face, or voice is saying something else. That's why it is essential for us to understand our own communication style. Effective leadership is dependent on good communication.

For some of us, it is difficult to take an objective look at ourselves. Often we are unaware of how others perceive us. We may be blinded to the fact that we come across as rigid, inflexible, overbearing, or demanding. From our perspective, we are just trying to do our job. Every leader needs at least one trusted friend who will honestly and lovingly help her discover her blind spots.

Because we do our best work when we foster a team spirit, ask the Lord to help you be flexible, positive, open, and supportive. Mutual support is crucial to the success of an organization and the effectiveness of a leader.

In his book, *Christian Leadership*, Bruce Powers illustrates four communication styles: pleaser, controller, avoider, and life-giver. Try to identify your style.

The *pleaser* is one who assumes the other person has more to contribute, therefore makes few contributions of her own. More specifically, this person will probably agree with whatever is suggested rather than risk upsetting someone.

The *controller* often tries to impose or sell her own point of view with little regard to alternate views. Because she believes her ideas are best, she discourages interaction.

The *avoider* is not interested in new approaches and assumes nothing can be done. Often she avoids dealing with issues to protect herself from involvement or commitment.

The *life-giver* encourages communication and exploration of ideas. She is willing to contribute ideas but does not assume she is right.

Obviously, life-giving communication is ideal. The style is open, direct, and clear. It is easy to trust life-giving communicators because you know where you stand and you feel good in their presence.

If you are presenting yourself in a positive light, others will welcome the opportunity to work with you. Not only will they take pride in your leadership, relationships will be easy, free, and non-threatening.

The way we perform our task

Make no small plans; they have no power to move men's hearts.
Unless our proposals are bold, they will be ineffective
—Elton Trueblood

There came a time in my life when I earnestly prayed: "God, I want your power!" Time wore on and the power did not come. One day the burden was more than I could bear. "God, why haven't you answered that prayer?" God seemed to whisper back this simple reply, "With plans no bigger than yours, you don't need my power."   —Carl Bates

The third component of our image as a leader is the way we perform our task. If you want to really know about a leader, ask those who work with her. Does she carry her fair share of the work load? Does she have a positive attitude about the work? Is she willing to pitch in on even the most menial tasks when a deadline is approaching? Does she accept blame for mistakes? Does she share rewards and praise with her co-workers?

What about the quality of your work? Are you a maintenance worker, doing business as usual? Does your leadership reflect a desire for excellence? One of the greatest temptations facing Christian leadership today is complacency. Maintaining the status quo is much easier than challenging the process. It doesn't require as much energy or commitment to keep things afloat as it does to address perceived needs and problems.

What do you want to see happen in your church? In your organization? In the lives of individuals? If you are going to be the kind of leader needed today, you must dream boldly and ask boldly for God's help and His blessing. Remember that He is able to do so much more than we can ever ask for or even think of.

Set your imagination free. Force yourself to move beyond the status quo. Be open. Be flexible. Allow God's Spirit to stretch your dreams into realities. When you do, your leadership will be contagious.

From your perspective
1. If your picture was on the front of a leadership magazine, how would you describe a leader from looking at the picture?

2. Reflect on the idea of God-Esteem. From what source do you gain and/or measure your esteem?

3. What are some areas of your leadership image which need special attention? How will you do this?

4. What do you want to happen in your organization, church, and community? How will you help this happen through your leadership?

The many faces of leadership
Katharine Bryan

A common expression of women in some areas of the South, and perhaps beyond, is "I must put on my face." This comment refers to the appropriate makeup the woman wears and the fact that few people outside the closest circle of family and friends will see this woman without her "face" on.

Leadership does not put on a face. Recognizing the many faces of leadership will free a woman to acknowledge the unique "face" with which she has been gifted. It will also enable her to affirm faces of leadership as she interacts with others. The face is not a mask to cover the real person. The faces of leadership are the evidences of those qualities which have so permeated the life of a woman they enable her to live, move, and have her being in a natural, unaffected way.

Role models

An effective leader operates from a stance of good followship. This is the *modus operandi* of servant leadership; the servant by the very nature of her position is a follower. She takes direction and responds to the leadership of another.

In order for a leader to be all she is intended to be, she must be constantly aware of following the One she ultimately serves. The Lord has gifted her and He will direct and instruct. He desires the very best of His followers. The leader's face must reflect her Creator and her chosenness. "You did not choose Me, but I chose you" (John 15:16 NASB).

The effective leader recognizes her Master and acknowledges her willingness to be a follower under His divine guidance. She also recognizes she is a product, to some degree, of those human leaders who have influenced her. Indeed, as followers we learn to be leaders!

Unique faces of leadership emerge. Individuals distinguish themselves by the realm of influence exerted. Any leader can name quickly those persons who influenced her. And a leader, at any given moment, is a combination of leadership traits learned from those who have had an impact on her life. These influences, added to the person's gifts, skills, experiences, and opportunities, become the framework for another unique face of leadership.

The influence of the role model widens in the classroom where teachers teach as they have been taught. An Acteens leader who provides guidance, direction, stability, and missions awareness for a group of girls is also providing a model for relationships, commitment, and consistency. As the girls mature and step into leadership roles, the model provided by that Acteens leader, perhaps years earlier, becomes evident in the next generation.

The effective mission study leader seeks resources to create an atmosphere of world awareness for the members of Baptist Women. She utilizes good teaching methods in providing a variety of stimuli for the senses. She seeks to involve the learner in seeing and hearing about missions, as well as touching, tasting, and even smelling. As a new leader is approached for mission study, her response may be influenced by the role model provided by the previous leader.

As individuals, we are able to copy others. You watch another person doing a task, carrying out the responsibilities of a particular office, and relating in different situations. You may be unaware of any influence she has on your life. Yet given similar circumstances, positive or negative, you will draw on the model observed.

A role model's influence may extend over a period of years; leadership is exerted across several developmental stages.

Each opportunity of working, parenting, relating, training, serving, and speaking becomes an opportunity for someone (or many someones) to be influenced by a role model.

Nurturer

Springtime provides a challenge to some of us as we see plants for sale. We dream of what our home or office will look like with beautiful plants growing and blooming. There is a certain amount of fantasy in thinking of a well-shaped, healthy plant with good color and appropriate behavior. (Appropriate behavior means blooming at the right time with the right color!)

Perhaps you give in to your impulse, accept the challenge, and purchase a plant at the local produce stand. What do you have? Carefully ensconced in a four-inch, green plastic container, your new plant has perhaps one fragile twelve-inch stem with five small leaves. The little stake of directions which accompanies your plant pictures profuse blooms and infers that, with proper care, what you see now in the plastic pot has the potential of becoming all it was meant to be.

You don't envision the plant **as it presently exists** in the entry way of your home, gracing your antique table for all to admire. What you envision is **what it can become** occupying that space. And you set in motion to help it become!

You check the soil and add some rich nutrients, not too much, just the right amount. You choose a spot with the proper light, and water the plant at designated intervals. You monitor it regularly to ensure it gets enough light and water for growth. When it begins to grow, you place it in a larger container in order for the roots to grow deep and spread out for balance. You adjust fertilizer, water, and light as growth continues.

A bud appears, and you watch expectantly. Carefully, you protect the small bud from the violence of your vacuum cleaner or the energetic inquiry of your children. More buds appear and burst into blooms. It becomes a strong plant in a good environment.

You no longer have to provide the same meticulous care. Your plant still needs water and light; however, it can probably handle the trauma of being "attacked" by the runaway wheels of your four-year-old's favorite truck.

Now you notice some small, tender, fragile shoots coming from this healthy plant. Could it be they are ready for the four-inch plastic pot?

A leader may identify potential in others using their gifts in some significant way. She may imagine how someone she has led could influence and penetrate worlds beyond her reach, and she assumes the role of nurturer.

The nurturer *assumes* growth will take place. She sets about to encourage, to provide opportunities, to give time, to risk new avenues of exposure, and to place the one with potential in ever-widening circles of influence. The nurturer is careful to maintain balance in growth with opportunities. She knows that too many opportunities which don't result in appropriate growth will cause unhealthiness. The nurturer is willing to try various formulas, seeking always for the one being nurtured to discover the very best for herself.

The nurturer is careful of bumps and rough spots where there is fragility; however, she knows maturity in leadership requires the ability to handle the difficulties which inevitably come. The nurturer/leader does not desire for the one nurtured to become just like her. Rather, she desires for the one nurtured to reach her full potential, and to acknowledge her giftedness. The leader prays for her to have confidence. The nurturer leads the future leader to be more aware of her Creator and His constant nurture. In this process, the leader-to-be becomes less aware of the person who saw potential and was willing to be a part of the Creator's process.

"May your roots go down deep into the soil of God's marvelous love; and may you be able to feel and understand . . . how long, how wide, how deep, and how high his love really is; and to experience this love for yourselves" (Eph. 3:17b-19 TLB).

Mentor

A walk through the corridors of a teaching hospital will bring you in contact with a beautiful scene: an older physician surrounded by a group of young residents who are observing experience at work. The leader has been in practice for years. The residents, having completed medical school and armed with their coveted degrees, are being mentored by the older physician. She has seen death many times over, yet she has also experienced miracles in the healing process. She envisions more miracles through the lives of the young physicians.

A father and mother have managed the family business for years since assuming leadership from their parents' generation. They know the ins and outs of the business, what has been successful and what has not. They can recall both good times and bad, and there is pride in their success. They still have dreams and visions for the future. When they see a natural interest on the part of a son or daughter, they begin to share the intricate workings of the business. They share secrets of the trade which have helped them realize success. They share the pitfalls which have the capacity to snare even the best in the business. They talk of hard work and commitment. They talk of the benefits, the serendipitious experiences which have been theirs along the way. They begin to give to their children some of the responsibility. They allow them to grow into the business.

Perhaps the young resident does not agree totally with the diagnosis or the prescribed treatment for the patient. The son or daughter may not "buy into" how the family business is operated. However, the mentors, those who are willing to teach others, are aware of that risk. The mentor is aware she may be training someone who will far excel anything she has ever attempted to do, and with a tinge of mixed emotions, she stays steady in the task of mentoring.

A mentor/leader is willing to listen to the questions which by their very nature often elicit defensiveness. To a mentor, questions are opportunities for evaluation and personal restructuring of methods and responsibilities.

The mentor/leader is teacher, role model, and nurturer. She helps instill respect for the task, its history and purpose, the future possibilities. The mentor assumes the role of communicating how one particular part relates to the whole of the organization. She allows her experience to make tracks which the one being mentored may follow. She knows that there are no boundaries for the size of the tracks; the ones which follow may completely cover up her original steps.

The mother who takes time to help her small child place pieces of cookie dough on the baking sheet is mentoring. The experienced, capable Girls in Action leader who urges an inexperienced young woman, in whom she sees potential, to join her as she plans for and works with young girls is a mentor. The Baptist Woman president who shares with another how she plans and prepares to preside is a mentor.

By definition a mentor is a "wise, loyal advisor." Wisdom is necessary as the mentor/leader decides when to listen and when to share. A mentor is wise in knowing how much time is needed for a particular project. A mentor is loyal to the one being mentored. She accepts less than perfection and she offers respect. She is loyal during the more difficult times of learning, not willing to give up on someone in whom she has invested time and emotional energy. As advisor, the mentor draws carefully on her own knowledge and skills. She is able to share with a sensitivity to timing and in appropriate amounts.

A mentor is a teacher par excellence. Mentoring must not become a lost art! Scripture gives beautiful examples of mentors in both the Old and New Testaments. What would it have been like to have Priscilla, Naomi, Paul or Jesus as a mentor? Who mentored you? Have you found an occasion to express appreciation? Who are you mentoring?

Administrator

There is a sense of security and a feeling that all is well when things are organized and running smoothly. This is recognized immediately as one walks into the committee meeting, seeks a certain item in a store, attends an event, or visits in a home. An administrator has been at work!

Churches and families have administrators as do corporations and organizations. Schools and hospitals seek good administrators to be in charge, to get things done. In any of these arenas, there are individuals who have assigned tasks. There are officers with organizational responsibilities or job assignments. There may be numerous people doing superb jobs, with specific goals and high motivation. It is the administrator/leader who has the ability to take these individuals with their own unique skills and responsibilities toward a common goal. Without her, there may be fragmentation and a sense of disunity even when individuals are doing their jobs. This face of leadership is gifted in bringing order out of chaos.

The administrator/leader sees a broader picture. She grasps purpose and sees individuals as being a part of something larger than their specific responsibility. She operates from the axiom *the whole is greater than the sum of its parts.*

The administrator/leader recognizes the unique gifts and skills of individuals and seeks to give people responsibilities which will utilize those gifts. She does not manipulate. She accepts her gift of administration and encourages others to be the doers. She is aware the doers will receive the credit for a job well done. The administrator/leader will receive strong personal satisfaction from knowing the task was done well by someone else. However, an effective administrator/leader is willing to do even the most menial task.

The administrator understands the art of delegation and is comfortable with letting go of major responsibilities. She is able to delegate authority as well as responsibility. However, she knows she is ultimately responsible for the tasks being done. She gives overall direction. She sees where the strengths lie, and she is aware of weak links. She strives to place people in positions where their strengths will be magnified and where their weaknesses will be irrelevant.

The administrator/leader affirms the members of the team. She is firm in decisions, and she seeks to do the right thing in each situation. She respects each person and does not want the task to be of higher value than the person doing the work.

Warren Bennis has said, a manager does things right, a leader does

48

the right thing. The ideal administrator/leader strives to do the right thing while doing things right. The administrator/leader establishes priorities while being aware it will never all get done. She communicates these priorities to all who are a part of the team and guides each to give energy toward the established priorities. The role of a leader who is labeled a director usually carries with it strong administrative functions. Job responsibilities will include words such as coordinate, organize, communicate, and represent. The administrator/leader directs the organization, but more importantly, she directs the people who make the organization successful in fulfilling its intended mission.

This face of leadership is the glue which binds the organization, its many facets, and its members together. It is the glue because incorporated in the administrator/leader are basic elements needed for any successful group:

- •Trust—the quality out of which the team functions, knowing what to expect and what is expected.
- •Effectiveness—enabling each person to reach her personal and corporate potential.
- •Quality—"a fine sense of one's obligations."
- •Vision—seeing beyond the present horizon.
- •Communication—providing power for the individual with information that must not be hoarded.

Warren Bennis and Burt Nanus in their book, *Leaders*, liken the administrator to an orchestra conductor. Work is done by the people in the group, just as music is produced by the orchestra. The conductor, like the administrator, serves the crucial role of seeing that the performance has coordination, proper pacing, and desired impact. The administrator calls for the best from all involved. She lives out the admonition "Let all things be done decently and in order" (1 Cor. 14:40 KJV).

Instructor

Priscilla was the beautiful teacher who instructed Apollos; other instructors are mentioned in the Scriptures, among them Paul, Deborah, Eunice, and Lois. Yet as we read Scripture and are willing to use our imaginations, many faces could emerge as teachers who are never named. Almost any task is done in a particular way because of instruction. Early childhood is full of "let me show you how." The inquisitive older child is constantly demanding, "Show me how." The realization is clear; each of us is the product of many hours of instruction, both direct and indirect, and countless numbers of instructors.

In a small, ill-equipped room, three children gather for Mission Friends. The leader carefully selects a story to tell. She asks the children questions. She encourages them to ask questions about the story. When she senses they understand the story, she relates it to what the children know in their own home and community. They talk about what they can do. She prays with the children for the things which they care about.

A similar scene takes place week after week. The leader does not seek recognition. In fact, very few people in the church are aware of what is happening.

Years pass, and the children grow up. A missionary is the guest of the church. The place of service for the missionary is announced. The "child grown up" recognizes the country and deeper interest is stirred. As she attempts to recall how or why she already knows about this country and perhaps even this missionary, the face of her teacher from years before, flashes across her mind. She realizes that impressions from stories told years before have lodged in her mind and on her heart. She has been affected for life by an instructor/leader.

The instructor is a face of leadership which many may claim although they may be hesitant to acknowledge it as a leadership role. This statement is familiar, "I can't lead. I just teach." Many women perform the multitude of tasks in guiding children in the home without recognizing the instructor/leader role they assume.

Countless numbers of women prepare diligently and go into a Sunday School class to teach, unaware of their leadership role in the lives of class members. A member of Baptist Young Women assumes the task of teaching the mission study for a particular emphasis in her group. She has expressed strong feelings regarding her inability to lead the group as an officer; however, she is eager to read and share with the group information she gleans from her resources. She may be surprised to learn she is fulfilling a leadership role. She is an instructor.

Instruction may be limited to one person informing another regarding a certain task. It may be confined to a young person showing a parent a new skill and assisting the parent until the skill is mastered. Or teaching may occur because of a need identified by a mission action group whose members teach English-as-a-second-language classes, personal hygiene, nutrition, prenatal care, or how-tos in a multitude of areas. The instructor may lead a class of 100 in Bible study, or she may tell a mission story to the three children on Wednesday night!

Authority

Leadership often emerges in the form of authority. If a crisis arises, someone in authority assumes the leadership role. Elected officials, teachers in the classroom, and parents have roles of authority and, as a result, become the identified leader in another person's life.

Authority is defined as rightful power. Authority figures are those who are perceived to have rightful power over others. The only way the authority/leader role can be reconciled with servant leadership is through the concept of *rightful power*. A woman in authority with the power to make decisions, to speak for the organization, to preside at a meeting, or to delegate responsibility can do so with the "servant towel" resting naturally over her arm. She uses her rightful power for discernment. She has wisdom and imparts it appropriately.

The authority/leader has the rightful power to make hard decisions. She also has the power to bear burdens of confidentiality, of interruptions, of pain and even of purpose for the organization.

The authority/leader is visible. When asked, "Who is really in charge here?" all fingers point to her. The authority/leader identifies problems and finds people to solve them. She moves the situation from chaos to order, from dead center into a constructive process. The rightful power invested in authority makes this possible.

Authority may come by virtue of one's specialized knowledge or expertise. In some areas of work and particularly some areas of ministry, expertise may be required but non-experts may also participate. These helper look to the expert for guidance. The attitude of the authority should not be one of superiority, but of teamwork.

The authority/leader with a servant heart can be one of the most positive forces for a group. The leader who assumes responsibility for a group of Acteens Activators planning a trip many miles from home is an authority/leader. She has the opportunity of nurturing, training, and mentoring. She is the authority and power for decisions, discernment, and discipline. Not only will the girls see her as a fellow servant working with them in Vacation Bible School, but they will also see her as the person with authority in dealing with crisis.

To paraphrase Sophocles, "Power shows the woman."

Dictator

History does not lack in stories of dictators. Although they wielded tremendous power during their reigns, they garner little respect from historians. However, the number of people who will follow the dicta-

51

torial leader is countless. Contrary to popular belief, dictatorship is not a totally negative form of leadership. The woman who is elected to a leadership position and desires to make radical and immediate changes in an organization may accomplish this by dictating what, how and when the process is to take place.

A dictator may be the kind of leader needed when the task is repetitive, of short duration, or mechanical. When others' investment of time and energy could be better used, a dictator can be effective in short-term leadership.

The dictator/leader does not seek counsel or advice on a consistent basis. Often advice sought is a manipulative move in order to implement a preconceived plan or process.

The dictator is task oriented and must give direct instructions in order for the tasks to be accomplished. She is more concerned for the task than for the persons involved who might be affected. She is highly motivated, usually abounds in energy, and seems indestructible. The dictator often leaves an organization or group if she is not successful in enlisting followers who will follow direction unquestioningly or who want ownership in the project or event.

The dictator serves well where followers are not interested in ownership, and want to be told explicitly what to do. A dictator is effective when there is little emotional investment by those who follow.

The face of leadership called dictator does wield power. Her unwavering control, her intensity, and her tenacity are all powerful tools. These characteristics, when used appropriately, are dynamite in a leader. A dictatorial style provides speed but little, if any, flexibility. The end project or product from a dictator carries the sole signature of the leader: It looks like her; it sounds like her; and it functions like her. Most dictators do not train others; therefore, when the dictator is not available, no one can take her place. This leaves the organization solely dependent on her leadership.

Dictators do serve as role models; however, they do not serve well as a team member. The dictator/leader's style is cramped by a process which includes others, especially if there is approval necessary before action can begin. The dictator/leader can accomplish tasks and get them done quickly. The effectiveness of her leadership depends on the receptiveness of others to follow her unique style.

Leadership indeed has many faces. Each woman is gifted to lead in at least one arena of life. The nurturer who quickly affirms, encourages, and prods another is in a unique leadership role. The woman who takes an Acteens member "under her wing" during the roller-coaster years of emotional maturing, who listens, and who gives tough love through healthy discipline is an authority leader practicing nurturing.

To observe any leader is to see a unique combination of the faces of leadership. Those faces are a reflection of other leaders—a previous generation reproduced anew. They may have been parents, teachers, organizational leaders or even job supervisors. Each one has made an impact on those she sought to lead.

Leadership, in whatever face it is seen, must have some foundational tenets to which those who follow can respond. The authoritarian, dictator, nurturer, administrator, mentor, instructor, and role model would do well to heed these reminders for Christian leaders from Max DePree, author of *Leadership Is an Art*:

A belief that each person is made in the image of God has enormous implications for leaders.

An understanding of the diversity of gifts God has given people is a crucial step toward trust.

A belief that God has provided a population mix becomes an accountability factor for leaders.

A belief that every person brings something to a group will require us to maintain an inclusive stance in our leadership.

From your perspective

1. Who have been the nurturers in your life? In your leadership roles? How has this been done? Have you expressed your gratitude to them?

2. Who are you nurturing presently?

3. Identify your leadership style. What are its strengths? What are the hazards of this style?

4. Are the leaders of your organizations serving as mentors? How is this being done?

Who will follow in your footsteps?

Barbara Curnutt

♡

Recently I received a call from Lynette, a friend who had accepted the position of WMU director in a large urban association. As we talked, her excitement and vision for the new year began to spill over into our conversation. In listening, I learned that every leadership position under her had been filled quickly with capable, creative women.

How was Lynette able to secure such a strong team, and seemingly so easily? These are the 1990s. Women are being bombarded by increasing demands on their already busy lives. Today's woman must be selective in the commitments she makes.

Those who forecast trends tell us that many contemporary women have decided that commitment is not in their best interest. It limits their independence and personal freedoms. How did Lynette defy all the odds? Let's uncover her secret.

In an attempt to satisfy my own curiosity, I began to probe. I discovered two basic factors. Lynette knew the kind of women she needed and wanted around her, and the women who agreed to serve knew and respected Lynette.

Could it be that these women *selected* Lynette as their leader? Could it be they chose to follow Lynette because she demonstrated qualities they expected in a leader? Followers are picky people. They have a right to be. It may very well be true that leadership is in the eye of the follower. How followers perceive a leader is far more important than how the leader views herself.

The way a leader is perceived by her followers will greatly influence the kind of leadership team she is able to build around her. If people recognize in a leader qualities they appreciate and respect, they will more readily commit to follow her.

Successful leadership is not only about leaders; it is also about followers. A person can dream, plan, and organize all day long, but if others are not willing to follow, it becomes a solo performance.

Leadership is an interdependent, mutual relationship. We serve as leaders only at the point of our gifts. We serve as followers at the point of others' gifts. It is a relationship that places individuals and individuality above positions and duties. It is a mutual relationship based on trust, open communication, and respect for differing gifts.

Be a discipler of leaders

As a leader, one responsibility is to disciple potential leaders. Your task is broader than simply keeping positions filled. It involves fostering a climate in which future leaders are called out and nurtured.

Potential leaders are more likely to explore their calling and experiment with their gifts when they are in a challenging environment where good leadership skills are modeled. As you practice good leadership principles, you will be creating a climate for growth of new leaders.

An effective leader/discipler is one who empowers others to discover and exercise their God-given gifts. The result? Service to God. Few responsibilities will be more challenging to you as a leader than the investments you make in the lives of your followers.

Jesus provided the greatest leadership model for us. Consider the way He took a diverse group of, unexceptional men, communicated His vision, and empowered them for service. With less than three years of training, Jesus' disciples performed an extraordinary feat: They nurtured and developed the church which Jesus Christ established.

Think about the women in your church or association. Are there some potential leaders? In what ways are you leading them to mature in His likeness? How can you lead them to be empowered for His service?

Providing a climate of trust may be the first step toward empowering your followers. Trust is the emotional glue that binds followers and leaders together. It cannot be demanded; it must be earned. Sensitive leaders know that while their position gives them authority, their behavior earns them respect. Predictability and consistency add to a leader's credibility. Leaders who build trusting relationships with their followers feel comfortable with them. They are open to differing views and opinions. Without trust, leaders appear threatened and hold tight control over their followers. In an atmosphere of trust, followers will feel secure in exercising their gifts. They will be more willing to risk failure in a safe, predictable environment.

A second step in empowering followers involves fostering a healthy team spirit. A team spirit is enhanced when all are involved in planning and problem solving. Create opportunities for interaction and sharing of ideas. Show that you respect each person's individuality and unique contribution. Potential leaders will blossom if they know you value their input and have confidence in their opinions.

Finally, followers are empowered when the leader gives her power away. The more a follower feels that she can influence the organization or group, the greater her satisfaction and productivity will be. When leaders share their power, followers feel more loyalty and are more committed to carrying out their duties and responsibilities.

Delegate important tasks to your followers and let go. Provide autonomy and authority with assignments. If you truly want to develop leaders, allow individuals freedom to make decisions without checking with you on every detail.

Good leadership perpetuates good leadership. It empowers others: building trust, fostering team spirit, giving power away. The right kind of leader brings out the best in others; she develops future leaders.

Look at the big picture

Before enlisting others in leadership roles, it is important to look at the big picture. Begin with the purpose of the organization. Why does it exist? What is its purpose? Why would a woman want to invest her time, gifts, and abilities through this particular avenue of service?

Because a woman's time is so valuable, she must see the credibility and worthiness of the organization before she will agree to serve. She must realize the significance of the job she is being asked to accept.

If you were explaining the purpose of your organization to a prospective leader, what would you say?

Next, consider priorities. What do you hope to accomplish through the organization this year? What are your goals for the next two to three years? Knowing where you are headed and what you plan to achieve will influence who is selected to serve on the leadership team. Expressed priorities will also affect a new leader's decision to serve.

Once the organization's purpose and priorities have been determined, you are ready to identify specific leadership needs. Specify and prioritize your needs. Then think through the kinds of leaders that you need.

Look for the right kind of people

As you think about the positions you are seeking to fill, consider the kind of people who would best serve your purpose. Who are you looking for? Be careful to focus on the person and not solely on the position.

When longtime Dallas Cowboys coach Tom Landry drafted players, his first goal was to find the best athlete. The position was secondary to the ability of the athlete.

When Lynette was asked to describe the kind of women she was seeking for the associational leadership team, it was evident that positions were secondary to gifts and skills possessed by the women enlisted to serve. Look at the characteristics she sought:
- willingness to do things differently;
- gifts in the specific area in which asked to serve;
- ability to be a team player;
- commitment to missions as a priority;
- willingness to secure a prayer partner.

What qualities should you look for in recruiting leaders? Let's examine some possibilities, realizing our list is not a comprehensive one. Search for women who have these qualities:
- committed to the Lord, to His church and His mission;
- gifted in the area of position in which they are being asked to serve;
- excited about learning;
- team players;
- flexible and adaptable to unexpected circumstances;
- open to new ideas and new ways of doing things;
- risk takers;
- confrontive in a healthy manner when necessary;
- dependable and trustworthy;
- focused, but not so intense that they cannot laugh at themselves and with others.

Although it may not be possible to find people who possess all ten qualities, you should not be deterred from aiming high. Often we miss opportunities to secure quality leaders because of mediocre expectations. Sometimes we are simply too timid to ask; we are afraid they will decline. If you believe in the value and purpose of the organization, be bold in your expectations.

Enlist the right people

Once leadership qualities and needs have been determined, you are ready to recruit. The best place to begin is on your knees in prayer. Patiently seek the Holy Spirit's guidance and direction in enlisting the right people. He, who knows your needs, has gifted people to meet those needs.

With the assurance of God's presence and activity in the enlistment process, securing leadership does not have to be a drudgery, nor does it have to be intimidating. It can even be fun as you help women unwrap and use their gifts. Recruiting can be a tremendously rewarding experience when gifts of the individual are successfully matched with the tasks of a particular ministry.

Although every Christian is unique in her giftedness, each shares the need to utilize her gifts in meaningful ways. You may be the catalyst linking gifts to opportunities of service.

Understanding some of the reasons women choose to volunteer will help you recruit with confidence. For most of us, the reasons are basically the same:

•desire to serve God and others;
•need to apply God-given gifts and talents;
•need to find self-fulfillment;
•longing to invest in a worthy cause;
•desire to make a significant contribution by influencing decisions.

When you see yourself as an enabler, empowering others to find their place in God's kingdom, you will be freed to approach prospective leaders unapologetically.

Start with a clean slate. Avoid the common pitfall of recycling leadership without good reason. This is not to say a woman should not serve again after fulfilling her original commitment. Rather, she should be invited to serve because she is the best choice for the task.

Organizations and individuals alike will suffer when leadership is overused. Even the best leaders need times of rest and refreshment from the demands of leadership. So make clear your intentions of viewing every leadership position anew and afresh.

In looking for leaders, be careful not to limit your focus to only those people who readily come to mind. Many make the mistake of selecting individuals they know and like rather than choosing people most suited for the job. When we enlist people just like ourselves, we duplicate our own strengths and weaknesses.

Use as many sources as possible when seeking new leaders. If you have access to spiritual gift inventories or interests surveys, use them. Ask about people who have recently moved into your area. Discover their interests, skills, and experience.

Look for natural leaders, people who get things done. Perhaps they are not currently involved in your organization, but they might be with the right opportunity. The invitation to serve may be all that is needed.

You may want to publicize your needs through newsletters, announcements, bulletin boards, or special presentations. The risk in making a public declaration of needs is that unqualified people will volunteer. The advantage is that qualified volunteers, who may have been overlooked, might respond if they are made aware of the needs.

Prospective leaders should be contacted personally. If possible, a personal visit is ideal. A pre-arranged visit allows for open, unhurried dialogue. It also communicates the significance you place on the job.

As you approach potential leaders, be positive and honest. Women deserve to know what is expected of them before making commitments. They also deserve to know how you plan to equip them for the job.

Because women lead busy, demanding lives and value their discretionary time, they may be hesitant to make long-term commitments of any kind. And yet, they want to serve. If you encounter a reluctance to accept long-term commitments, think about different options:

•Shared leadership is one approach in which two women serve as co-leaders.

•Short-term leadership allows women to make monthly or quarterly, rather than year-long, commitments.

•Project-oriented leadership involves women in specific projects with specific time frames.

•Group leadership is an option for women who prefer to serve as a member of a planning committee.

•Apprenticeship is another option that provides on-the-job training for women who are hesitant to assume full responsibility. In an apprenticeship, an experienced leader serves as a mentor to another.

If you continue to come up empty-handed in attempting to fill a position, try restructuring the job. Maybe the expectations are unrealistic. Perhaps women simply are not willing to commit to the responsibility under present circumstances. You may need to rethink the job.

Just because something has always been done one way, you should not rule out the possibility of change. Neither should change be instituted simply for the sake of change. If change is warranted, be careful to remain focused on your purpose.

Remember that although a person may volunteer with the best intentions, she may not be the best person for the job. Making wrong choices can be more damaging than experiencing leadership vacancies. Wrong choices are often difficult to undo and destructive in the process. If a vacancy becomes an obstacle, secure a qualified interim leader or consider restructuring the job. Never fill a vacancy in panic. Prayerfully and patiently wait for God's person to emerge in God's time.

Your job is not over yet
If your focus has been strictly on filling a position, then your job is done when the position is filled. But if your emphasis is on the person who fills the position, your responsibility continues in discipling the person, helping her to grow in Christlikeness as a person and leader.

It is one thing to find the right leader; it is an entirely different matter to help her maintain productivity and commitment to her task. Those whose organizations have been hampered by frequent turnover in leadership understand this challenge. You know the stress and frustration this problem brings.

While it may not be possible to completely eliminate the "swinging-door" leadership syndrome, there are preventive steps you can take. Two key areas are training and affirmation. Both are crucial to a leader's sense of effectiveness and personal fulfillment.

Today one of the fastest growing phenomena in our culture is continuing education for adults. Evening and weekend classes are increasingly popular on some community college campuses. Adults are rearranging their lives in order to obtain new skills or improve existing ones. This rapidly growing trend seems to indicate the need and demand for quality continuous training.

Whether it is in the corporate world or in a church setting, the quality of work a woman is able to do is inseparably tied to the training and preparation she receives. Leadership training is so important, consideration should be given to a year-round plan.

The obvious place to begin is with new leader orientation. Often we make the mistake of assuming a new leader knows more than she does. Maybe she has held similar positions in the past. Perhaps she is a naturally gifted leader, so we assume she has all the answers. Never assume past experience will suffice as leadership training. Organizational structure, goals, objectives, and special emphases may change from year to year. If a woman is not adequately equipped for the job, she will lack confidence, become easily discouraged, and eventually resign.

Do not forget your faithful, experienced leaders. Provide opportunities for them to receive fresh, new ideas and to renew their sense of call. Encourage them to attend associational or state training events.

Plan early for the six-month slump. Schedule a midyear refresher course that will rejuvenate and recharge your leaders. Make it inspiring, informative, and fun.

Think about providing opportunities throughout the year in which people with specific expertise are invited to meet with targeted groups. For example, a minister of youth might be asked to discuss issues and trends with youth leaders. Or a Christian counselor might be enlisted to help the entire group improve their relational skills.

As you envision a year-round leader training plan, be sure the basics are provided and then explore other possibilities. Whatever you do, keep it relevant and meaningful.

Another way to encourage leadership longevity is through consistent, credible affirmation. Pay attention. Know when leaders have done a good job and acknowledge their accomplishment, either publicly or privately. Affirmation will enable them to begin clarifying their gifts.

Take time to know your leaders. Learn to be thankful for their uniqueness. Then discover ways to show that you appreciate who they are as much as what they do.

Leadership development is cyclical, an ongoing process that focuses on people before positions, and power sharing rather than power hoarding. Above all it is a process that must be permeated with prayer.

From your perspective

1. What is your criteria for leadership?

2. Does your criteria match the vision you have for and needs of the organization? (Example: high expectation = creative vision; few criteria = little happening)

3. How does your organization enlist leaders?

4. What are some on-going training opportunities which could be offered for the women in your church?

What do you mean, a dynamic process?
Bobbie S. Patterson

―――――――――――――― ♡ ――――――――――――――

dynamic \di-nam-ik\adj 1 a: of or relating to physical force or energy, b: active 2 a: marked by continuous and usually productive activity or change, b: marked by energy, forceful.

process \pros-es\ noun 1 a: progress, advance, b: something going on, proceeding 2 a: a natural phenomenon marked by gradual changes that lead toward a particular result b: a series of actions or operations conducing to an end; a continuous operation

Leadership is a *dynamic process*. When we put the words *dynamic* and *process* together, we find that leadership is an active, forceful phenomenon leading to a particular result. It affects, risks, drives, inspires, threatens, supports. In leadership each person finds her own avenues of expression in involving others in accomplishing a goal or direction.

Leadership is a force that you and I can exert to influence major accomplishments in missions. The bottom line of missions leadership is to involve people, churches, and associations in leading lost people to accept God's plan of redemption. Leadership is a dynamic process of being a missions advocate in your spheres of influence.

Five descriptive phrases sum up leadership as a dynamic process.

1. Leadership is moving, not static.

Leadership produces action or forward movement rather than standing still. It arouses, affects, and compels others to action. In your mind contrast what it means for leadership to be moving rather than static. Leadership as a dynamic process is much more than a title or a position to which a person is elected. The title "Girls in Action leader" does not make a woman a leader in the truest sense of the word. She is only a leader when she takes appropriate actions and is a part of this dynamic process of being a leader.

Dynamic leadership means you are accomplishing something, proceeding toward an end. Dynamic leadership does not merely wait for something to happen. A Girls in Action leader will not influence the lives of girls for missions involvement by standing still. Rather, she influences them through actions—inspiring, motivating, planning, supporting, facilitating, modeling, and sharing.

Women have the tendency, indeed a great capacity, to give attention to and enjoy process. For most of us, the process is often more satisfying and significant than bringing closure to an activity. The *doing*, not getting the task *done*, is often what is most important and enjoyable. Therefore, *being* a Girls in Action leader rather completing a study of Indonesia or concluding a year of Missions Adventures is where she'll find her satisfaction.

Since most women leaders are action oriented and process centered, leadership as a dynamic process should come naturally to them. Capitalize on this female characteristic. Make the process of leadership vibrant and important for the cause of missions.

2. Leadership is active, not passive.

For most Christian women, leadership is a calling from the Lord and a ministry to be performed for Him. Therefore, dynamic leadership is not something passive that you wait to happen to you. Nor should you wait for someone else to tell you what to do. Leadership is active and intentional, which translates into influencing others and taking risks.

Consider the following list of qualities and judge for yourself whether these qualities are active rather than passive:
- A leader meets needs.
- A leader facilitates relationships.
- A leader facilitates personal growth.
- A leader models Christian living.
- A leader dreams, inspires, and supports.

•A leader takes courageous stands, often in the face of opposition.

•A leader manages conflict.

•A leader shares leadership.

Verbs such as *meets, facilitates, models, dreams, inspires, supports, takes stands,* and *manages* are action words. What actions can you take as a leader that would personify these qualities? What needs should you address? What relationships require your attention?

3. Leadership is a continuing process, not an end result.

Think in terms of leadership as moving and cyclical, rather than as a function with a specific beginning and ending time. Leadership often involves repetitious tasks.

As uncomfortable as the notion of continuing a repetitious job might be for you, consider the alternative. What if leadership ended at the conclusion of one task? While WMU promotes and encourages using project leaders for short-term assignments, those with a long-term commitment to our missions task form the backbone of WMU. Specific job assignments may vary from year to year, but the leadership influence continues. Staying with one job may bring the risk of boredom, but it offers unexpected rewards. Ask the Mission Friends leader who sees God's care for His children through the eyes of a four-year-old if she's willing to give up the joy and spontaneity of preschoolers. She may be tired or sometimes bored, but each week's adventure in Mission Friends brings a new opportunity to share God's love and care.

Have you ever watched a spider as she spins her web? Her activity is a steady process; the web may continue to grow or may need ongoing repairs. The spider rests, but the job awaits when she awakens. Think of a Navajo weaver as she steadily weaves patterns into her rug. A rug is completed eventually, but the process continues; a new project is begun when one rug is removed from the loom.

Perhaps you have stood on the shore and watched the ebb and flow of the tides. The movement of the water goes on and on, according to a never-ending pattern. Missions leadership continues. Planning, relating to others, influencing, implementing plans, and evaluating must be done over and over again.

4. Leadership is moving, not maintaining.

When leadership is dynamic, there is a plan or direction, and movement forward toward the accomplishment of a goal.

The opposite of movement is maintenance. When you only have the title *leader* by virtue of election to a position and you are in a maintenance mode—doing little that's productive and reaching no new goals—there may be little reason for you to retain the position. The same principle applies to organizations. When an organization is in a maintenance mode, it may need to go out of business.

Churches need dynamic leaders, leaders with a vision who will plan, set goals, give direction, and achieve results. A dynamic leader will keep the organization moving, accomplishing goals related to the cause which brought it into existence in the first place.

5. Leadership is practical, not theoretical.

Have you ever attended a conference or seminar where you listened intently and took voluminous notes, but six months later you could not identify even one change in your usual pattern in spite of the training?

Understanding the biblical principles or the theoretical concepts of leadership is not enough. Nor is simply having head knowledge about leadership traits, skills, and abilities adequate. Nor is training significant unless what you have learned about leadership is applied in practical ways.

For example, you may be capable of defining *nurturer*, writing an essay on being a *mentor*, or identifying specific steps on acting as an *encourager*. If you are not continually applying these understandings to your relationships, you are a "sounding brass or a tinkling cymbal" (1 Cor 13:1).

When you lead with practicality in mind, you can easily see the importance of the present. Of course, your past experiences and expectations of the future make an impact on who you are as a leader and how you lead. However, practical and dynamic leaders live and function in the present. They know that work must be done today, and they manage time effectively and efficiently to lead each day to the fullest.

How can you be dynamic?

It is one thing to talk about dynamic leadership, quite another thing to *be* a dynamic leader. How can you be a dynamic, forceful, energetic, and productive leader?

1. Discover and use your own style of leadership.

Some authorities on leadership categorize leadership types as dominant, influencing, steady, or capable. Others label leaders as achievers, facilitators, or influencers. Still others describe leaders as autocratic, democratic, or participatory in style. There is no one best way to describe leadership or one best style.

Some leaders influence through a strong personality and overt and dominant actions. Others lead through a quiet, yet persuasive manner.

Some influence and lead through steadiness or competence. Still others lead through force. Be assured, however, that the best leader is the one who recognizes the approach she favors and the effects her style will have on each situation she faces.

God has given each of us different qualities and characteristics. You and I are unique in the way that He has bestowed gifts, skills, talents, and leadership styles on us. In addition to the gifts and skills that are uniquely ours, we also possess some characteristics unique to women. Skill in nurturing and caring, developing relationships, and expressing joy and enthusiasm are frequently identified as female characteristics.

Two WMU directors come immediately to my mind as examples of women who relied on varying leadership styles. These women led effectively in different ways. Sarah was quiet, gentle, and caring; you might not have selected her as WMU director. However, she found her most effective leadership through her caring nature and ministry-oriented skills. She was skilled at finding and appropriating the gifts and abilities of other women in the missions enterprise. Church leaders, both men and women, as well as WMU members, loved and respected this gifted leader.

Delores possessed untold administrative and organizational skills. She led effectively through setting goals and direction for WMU, planning, organizing, building relationships. She persuaded other people to buy into and carry out the directions and goals she set. She also gained the respect, admiration, and love of church leaders, as well as WMU leaders and members.

Neither style of leadership evidenced in these women was better than the other. What was important was that each woman recognized and used her own style of leadership to its best result.

2. Pay your dues.

You do not automatically become a leader because you are elected to a position and bear the title *leader*. You earn the right to be acknowledged as a leader by the example you set and the actions you demonstrate. You must pay your dues.

What does it mean to pay your dues? It means being faithful to your responsibilities, being active and moving the organization forward: carrying out leadership tasks in quality ways; doing your best; striving for excellence; attending meetings where your presence is expected and important; dreaming and planning; setting directions and goals.

Paying your dues means speaking up; taking courageous stands for what you believe is right, even when the stand is controversial; being a missions advocate in every possible sphere of influence you have; developing and improving relationships; inspiring, encouraging, and motivating others; sharing leadership appropriately; seeing the potential in other persons; keeping a leadership position long enough to make a difference, yet knowing when to move off the leadership scene.

Perhaps, you can think of leaders who have influenced you by paying their dues. I know a leader who worked faithfully and regularly with preschoolers as a Mission Friends leader for many years. She paid her dues in a number of ways. She did so through regular and consistent planning. She took advantage of training opportunities to keep up-to-date and to improve her skills. She spent years building relationships with parents and other preschool workers. She prepared quality programs of study; she cared deeply about the learning environment she created for her preschoolers. Her loving and caring spirit was easily recognized as she worked patiently and faithfully with the children. She was also involved as an adult in missions experiences and participated fully as a team member in broader WMU planning.

What legacy did this Mission Friends leader leave? There are hundreds of persons influenced and trained under her leadership who are active in missions today because this leader paid her dues.

3. Do your homework.

Excellent preparation and participation on the part of the leader are two necessary aspects of doing one's homework. This is especially important if you are a woman leader who also works with male leadership. For example, you may be a WMU director who serves primarily with male leaders on the church council and in overall church programming. Also, you may work closely with the pastor as a missions advocate. Or, you may be an Acteens leader who works with the High School Baptist Young Men's leader and a male minister of youth to plan and implement coed missions activities for all youth in the church.

The woman leader who enters the male leadership arena must work doubly hard. Linguist Deborah Tanner addresses the problem of men and women in work relationships in *You Just Don't Understand*. Dr. Tanner asserts that men and women come to their jobs from different, but equally valid, perspectives. The keys are learning to communicate effectively and doing one's work extremely well. A woman can be a dynamic leader as she prepares well, participates fully as a team member, speaks up clearly and forcefully, relates positively to setting directions, and fulfills in a quality way any assignments which are hers.

68

4. Stay by the stuff.

The Old Testament story of David includes the occasion on which David and 400 of his soldiers put on their swords and went forth into battle. The story also indicates that 200 additional soldiers stayed with the supplies or "the stuff."

You will not always be up front as a dynamic leader. Sometimes you will have a less visible role. Regardless of where or how you are leading, you must "stay by the stuff" and remember your primary reason for being a missions leader. Stick with the main priorities—being a missions advocate and involving other people in missions.

For you, missions is the "stuff" you must stay by. Be faithful to the task of missions leadership. Your commitment to a person, Jesus Christ, and a cause, missions, will keep you going through the tense, difficult times of leadership as well as in the joyful, happy times.

Sometimes it's easier to take a leadership position and try it out for awhile. If it's more than we're really committed to, we can always quit, right? But staying by the stuff long enough to learn the job, develop the skills and abilities needed, and get experience equips one to better serve over the long haul. Again, the primary role of commitment to a task becomes clear.

Judy has served many years as an Acteens leader. She has been faithful in remaining in that place of service in spite of countless opportunities to change areas of service. However, feeling a strong sense of the Lord's call to relate to teenaged girls in missions, she has taken her responsibility seriously, stayed by the stuff, and influenced countless girls to grow and develop into missions-minded women.

How do I stay dynamic?

Becoming dynamic is not enough. The real test of leadership is to stay dynamic. It's easy to become complacent, get comfortable and stagnate. The challenge is to keep learning and developing, to stay fresh, vibrant, and dynamic as a leader. Four practical actions may help in your quest to not only *be*, but to *stay* a dynamic leader.

1. Maintain a sense of direction.

Take a closer look at missions and what it has to do with your sense of direction. God has a purpose of redeeming all creation to Himself. He has chosen to use His people known as Christians, in carrying out this mission. Therefore, it is imperative that each leader use her gifts and skills to help bring about this purpose, and to be a missions advocate in whatever sphere of influence she has.

A sense of calling and direction is vital to each kind of missions leadership, whether you are a Mission Friends leader influencing and shaping the lives of preschoolers, a Baptist Women mission action group leader involved in literacy missions, a Baptist Young Women president, or the director of Woman's Missionary Union in the church. Regardless of the area of leadership, you serve the God who called and equipped you for leadership.

A sense of direction is crucial, for there will be times of discouragement when nothing seems to be going right or getting accomplished. There will be times when other people do not cooperate. There will be times when the best laid plans do not succeed, when you are weary of the leadership role.

You must constantly and regularly reaffirm your call and commitment to the task. To do so may mean writing your goals and dreams in a private journal and periodically taking the time to reflect on how far you've come. Or you may need to plan an annual personal retreat for the opportunity to spend extended time in prayer. Some leaders keep their sense of direction by reading the success stories of other leaders who serve a role models. Of course, the ultimate inspirational reading comes from the Scriptures. Maintaining a sense of direction may mean reviewing the biblical basis of missions each year you continue in a leadership role in WMU.

2. Pace yourself and go with the flow.

Women tend to work at a steady pace, with small breaks and appropriate ups and downs. In that sense, there is an ecology of leadership. A healthy leader should learn to pace herself and go with the flow.

However, many women leaders are prone to take themselves too seriously. Women are sometimes easily offended or hurt, and discouraged when others let them down or the task gets difficult. These attitudes and responses are counterproductive to mature and dynamic leadership. If allowed to fester, such feelings may destroy leadership potential or influence.

Pace yourself; sometimes you need to wait, relax, and bide your time. Be patient; wait for the appropriate moment to take action.

In one large church, non-missions leaders seemed to oppose any program of missions education, let alone a quality program. Because of the pervasive influence of the church leaders, all programs for children, with the exception of Bible study, shut down for the summer months. However, two faithful directors, the Mission Friends director and the Girls in Action director, persisted in gentle, quiet, supportive leadership. Pacing themselves and waiting for the appropriate time paid off. This church now enjoys a healthy, year-round, quality missions education program for all ages.

3. Prepare yourself.

Preparation is key to staying dynamic and exercising quality leadership for missions.

Carefully review your job description. This will help you to fully understand your tasks and identify expectations others may have of you. I recall an experience when I served as Acteens director in a church. Early on, an Acteens leader from the previous year asked, "How do you plan to run Acteens?" I suspected strongly at that point that she had certain expectations of me based on previous experiences with Acteens directors. It was important for me to discuss these expectations, as well as many other areas of our work, with her.

The people who enlisted you as a leader may have expectations—to turn around a declining organization, to foster growth, or to improve relationships. Maybe the pastor, women who are not in WMU, or the church as a whole, have expectations of you. It is important to identify these expectations.

Take advantage of opportunities for study, training, or improvement. Not only is initial preparation for the job vital, but ongoing training provides new ideas and sharpens skills. You can complete some training individually—through observation, discussion with others, viewing videotapes, reading, and studying. Other training is available through seminars and conferences. Some training may come through trial and error on the job.

4. Be healthy.

Good health is essential in every area of life for you to stay dynamic. There are many dimensions to leadership health, physical and emotional, mental and spiritual.

You need to be healthy physically and emotionally to maintain a forceful and positive leadership influence. Good physical and emotional health includes proper diet, regular exercise, adequate rest, attitude adjustments when necessary, and a solid network of supportive relationships. Balance, regularity, and discipline are keys to maintaining good physical and emotional health.

As a leader you need to see physical and emotional health as spiritual issues. First Corinthians 3:16-17 says our bodies are temples of God. Thus, there is a stewardship of body, as well as a stewardship of time, gifts, skills, and abilities.

71

Mental health is also vital for a dynamic leader. You need to be growing and improving constantly as a leader. Keep up-to-date in skills, aptitudes, and abilities. Be missions literate and well informed about current missions events and happenings. Take advantage of formal opportunities to grow mentally. Be an avid reader. Take adequate time to reflect on the materials you have read and studied.

As a leader you must also be healthy spiritually. The state of your spiritual health has an impact on every other area of life. Maintaining a daily time of personal Bible reading and prayer, regular Bible study, private and corporate worship experiences, ongoing involvement and participation in your church, contact with other Christians, and exercising regular service and ministry opportunities—these are the necessary ingredients of spiritual health.

In order to lead dynamically, you must regularly and consistently be in a position to hear God's voice. You can do this as you keep the communications lines open through Bible reading, meditation, and prayer.

Leadership is a dynamic process. You are not a leader because you have a title, but because you are involved in an active, practical, methodical movement toward a specific goal. As a leader with a servant heart, that goal must be missions. How dynamic!

From your perspective

1. Identify at least three dynamic women leaders you know personally.

2. What is the major characteristic which makes them dynamic?

3. How have they influenced you? Have you told them?

4. What are some things you assume they do to enhance their leadership which are not seen publicly?

I have found the leader and she is I!

Barbara Joiner

—————————— ♡ ——————————

Anna Smith had not completed her first year at the helm of Merrymount's WMU before she was dreaming dreams. Leaders dream dreams. The really good ones have vision.

Anna had corralled and headed out a good group of leaders during the year, but she knew they were not all that they could be. She planned a retreat for the council and made an assignment to each woman—to insure that she would attend. She then enlisted the best teacher she could find to lead the retreat and teach *With a Servant Heart.*

Carefully, she checked and re-checked her plans. Everything was in order. Then Anna went one step further; she committed the retreat to the Lord. She found herself on her knees asking God to take the meeting and do with it as He willed. Anna was surprised at herself. She knew what she wanted from the meeting already, didn't she?

In fact, Anna had been unlike herself lately. Always supremely confident and self-assured, Anna had been searching. Ever since she had read *A Chance to Die, the Life and Legacy of Amy Carmichael* by Elisabeth Elliot, Anna had been different. She prided herself on her discipline; then she read that Amy Carmichael defined *discipline* as "that which I would not choose, but which Thy love appoints."

"Surely a person chooses; God's love doesn't choose for us," Anna reasoned. Yet, she wasn't as confident as usual.

On the day of the retreat, all went smoothly. Anna, of course, came loaded to the gills. Someone, probably Patsy, would forget her bed linens or snacks. Anna baked an extra cake and made one more casserole. Extra Bibles were tucked into her suitcase along with scads of pencils and paper. Anna was always prepared.

Brenda Lightfoot, the state WMU president, was the teacher Anna had chosen for the retreat. Brenda arrived at the conference center before Anna. That was a first! Brenda had already finished setting up for the first session and was bowed in prayer when Anna arrived.

Soon all the other women trooped in. Before long Brenda began the session. Anna had skimmed the book, but she had forgotten that two chapters covered the Biblical basis of leadership. "Ho hum," Anna thought. "Maybe it will go by quickly." She let her mind wander. Then several words broke through Anna's reverie: *servant, self-consecration, responsibility, love, slave.* Anna began to listen.

"The best model of servant leadership is found in the life of Jesus."

"Jesus begins to wash the disciple's feet."

"He humbled himself and became obedient to death—even death on a cross."

"Symbolized more by a towel and basin than a throne and a scepter."

Humility was not one of the distinguishing characteristics of Anna Smith. Her perfectly manicured nails were not made for basins, were they? Anna left the session. She found a quiet spot away from the crowd. She sought the Father, and found Him.

Nancy Carter saw Anna leave. Her heart rejoiced. She had worked with Anna for nearly a year and appreciated her forceful and thorough leadership. However, she sensed a vacuum in Anna's life and had prayed for her. In fact, it was Nancy who had given the Amy Carmichael biography to Anna. God had used that powerful book and the gifted teaching of Brenda Lightfoot. God had heard Nancy's prayers; tears of gratitude flowed down her face.

"I have so much to learn," cried Nancy. "I am not a leader like Anna."

The title of the next chapter of *With a Servant Heart* caught her ear. Nancy chuckled along with the other women. "What am I doing leading this parade? I didn't even plan to march!"

"Amen!" Nancy thought. "I certainly didn't plan to march, much less lead mission study!" Nancy had loved working with Mission Friends. She had not wanted to be a leader of women, her peers. Nevertheless, she had been shocked to discover how much she enjoyed her new responsibilities.

"I haven't done a bad job, "she concluded. She looked at the hand-out Brenda was distributing. As she glanced at the statements, she felt herself reeling. That first one: "Leadership requires a specialized spiritual gift." A year ago Nancy would have agreed and slunk from the room, but she had come to understand that all Christian women lead. And Nancy had led, with plenty of help from the Lord and from the dedicated Baptist Women at Merrymount. She breathed a sigh of relief and continued marking her handout.

There it was again. Number 5: "Every Christian woman is a leader."

"Is the Lord trying to tell me something?" Nancy pondered.

Nancy was delighted to see statement 7: "Leadership involves change." She knew God had changed her. In fact, the entire Baptist Women organization had changed during the year and grown as they learned together. "And I'm just a beginner," Nancy crowed to herself. Confidence, badly needed, was blooming in Nancy Carter.

Anna returned to the retreat just as Brenda began to focus on servant-hood in Chapter 4. Anna heard, "The Christian leader, empowered by the Holy Spirit, views her role from an entirely different frame of reference than her secular counterpart."

"Oh, yes," breathed Anna. She had just settled that matter with the Lord. Merrymount Baptist Church would see a newly empowered leader the following year.

Judy Nelson was deeply moved by the very same statement. She had used her formidable leadership skills to direct Baptist Women all year. "In fact," she reminisced, "I worked like a slave. I saw some things happen, but not what I expected. Now I know why. I continued to work as I did at the bank. Baptist Women are not employees. They are fellow laborers and leaders for the Lord! Forgive my prideful and haughty attitude, Lord."

Judy was so busy making vows to the Lord that she nearly missed the quote from Charles Swindoll's book *Improving Your Serve*. "The servant leader is a person who demonstrates transparent humanity, genuine humility, absolute honesty, and proper perspective for life."

Judy added her own conclusion to his quote: "Instead of directing like a bank vice president!"

Sara Mullins had been trying to resign her position for months. "If I were a real leader," she agonized, "I would just march up to Anna and announce my intentions. I don't even have what it takes to quit!"

When Sara accepted the job of Acteens director she had little confidence in her leadership skills. After working with dynamos like Anna and Judy, she knew she was no leader. However, Acteens had suddenly bloomed. Sara took none of the credit. "The Acteens leaders are simply great," she reminded herself. "All of them are good leaders. Well, maybe not June; she was not as dependable as a flea. But all of the others are much better than I. Meredith should take the director's job," Sara concluded.

Sara was actually an excellent leader, but because she was not like Anna or Judy, she saw herself as a failure. She was insecure and afraid; she despised herself.

Brenda's words broke through Sara's tortured thoughts. "You observe them and measure all that they are against all that you are," the teacher said.

"My goodness," Sara exclaimed to herself, "has Brenda Lightfoot been reading my thoughts?"

"Do you see yourself as capable and significant, uniquely created in God's image?" Brenda asked.

Sara found herself turning to Psalm 139 as requested. Brenda asked Sara to read aloud for the group. By the time she reached verse 9, Sara's heart was racing:

"If I take the wings of the dawn, if I dwell in the remotest part of the sea, even there Thy hand will lead me, and Thy right hand will lay hold of me."

Sara paused. The Lord had prepared Sara's heart to deal with own insecurities and inadequacies. Sara heard Brenda say, "In our weakness, God's power in made perfect."

"Some live life as people-pleasers."

"When our lives are lived in total dependence on God, we will experience peace and serenity . . ." Sara's pen raced. She underlined and wrote in margins of her book.

"Who is that leader in the mirror?" was the title of the chapter. "That face and those actions belong to me! I am that leader in the mirror!" Sara wanted to shout.

Instead, she listened. She heard ways to improve her image. "I'll begin walking every day. I'll make time. Desserts have to go. I'll ask Meredith to help me look at my blind spots. She's great friend." Sara was excited.

Then she heard Brenda present four communication styles: pleaser, controller, avoider, and life-giver. The life-giver encourages two-way communication and exploration of ideas.

"I do that!" Sara exulted to herself.

Then Brenda said, "Life-giving communication is ideal. Others welcome the opportunity to work with you."

Sara remembered, "I have all my Acteens leaders enlisted before anybody else has filled their spots. Maybe I'm doing something right."

When Brenda Lightfoot began Chapter 6, "The many faces of leadership," *Nell Mooney* rested her busy pen. Nell prided herself on her copious and correct minutes. "Minutes are not required for a retreat,"

Anna had told her. "Enjoy and learn."

Nell informed Anna that she had read *With a Servant Heart* as soon as it had become available. In fact, she had church study course credit before most people knew the book existed. To herself, Nell muttered, "I could have taught this book. Why did Anna ask Brenda to teach?"

Nell had noted in her minutes that Anna had left during the second chapter. Little did Nell realize that in her reading of the minutes Anna would react to that recording by giving a personal testimony of how God spoke through *With a Servant Heart.*

Nell also made mention of "Brenda's emotional teaching techniques: some participants were crying." Nell felt that sort of teaching was most unproductive.

As Nell paused in her note-taking, she heard, "Any leader can name quickly those persons who influenced her."

Everybody was given a "faces" chart. Nell looked at the categories: nurturer/leader, mentor/leader, administrator/leader, instructor/leader, authority/leader, dictator/leader.

"Who," Brenda asked, "helped you grow, carefully nurtured you, saw what you could be?"

Without hesitation, Nell wrote the name Maggie Richardson. Her mind went back many years to her GA leader. Nell's love for missions began under the influence of Mrs. Richardson. "I owe a lot to Mrs. Richardson," Nell admitted.

The next category was mentor/leader. "Easy," Nell thought as she jotted down Adell Smith. Mrs. Smith was the WMU director when Nell first joined the WMU council. Mrs. Smith knew WMU, loved missions, and took time to know Nell and to take her under her wing.

"She was my mentor," Nell thought.

As the exercise continued, Nell became aware of all those who had led her, but as Brenda concluded by reminding them of the debt they owed to the women who had led them, Nell had reached her own self-centered conclusion: "What a great job they did with me!"

Anna had observed Nell's interest. "Someone has touched Nell's life. That may be the key I need to unlock all her potential." However, as she saw the smug look come to Nell's face, Anna sighed. "Nell may not change, at least not right away. But she is dedicated and knowledgeable and so terribly efficient."

Jan Perkins had soaked up all the teaching from *With a Servant Heart*. She wanted to be a good leader. As Brenda began "Who will follow in your footsteps?" the seventh chapter of the book, Jan started getting excited. Leading Merrymount to pray for and give to missions had been a joy to her. The problem had been her unorthodox methods. No one else on the WMU council led as Jan did. Anna, in particular, did not understand Jan's need for so many people. Jan enlisted lots of people and gave them a lot a authority to do "their thing."

Brenda said, "A person can dream, plan, and organize all day long, but if other are not willing to follow, it becomes a solo performance."

"Yes!" Jan thought. Brenda continued, "If you are leading and nobody is following, you are just taking a walk."

Yes! Yes!" Jan thought. Every word Brenda spoke seemed to reflect Jan's beliefs. "Individuals and individuality should be placed above positions and duties."

"Yes! Yes! Yes!" Jan knew that was the way to go. She was a disci-pler of leaders. Anna had once said, "I feel as though I don't know who's really leading. You always have so many people involved."

Jan had smiled and agreed. "I need others to help me; mission support is a big task." Jan's methods had worked. She listened as Brenda out-lined the tenets of leader/follower cooperation.
•Create an atmosphere of trust.
•Foster a healthy team spirit.
•Give your power away.
"Exactly what I believe," Jan thought.

The different leadership options Brenda outlined struck a chord with Jan: shared leadership, short-term leadership, project leadership, group leadership, apprenticeships. Jan had tried most of them. She could hardly wait to try the rest.

Jan glanced at Anna. "Oh, Anna, get ready. I've only just begun."

Patsy Everheart let out her umpteenth sigh of the day. "At last, the final chapter," she moaned. "I though we'd never get through."

Patsy had planned a dinner party during the first several chapters. Then she had inventoried her winter wardrobe and pinpointed her greatest clothing needs. During the previous chapter she had actually filed her nails. Patsy had not "gotten into" *With a Servant Heart.*

She tried to concentrate on the last chapter, "What do you mean, a dynamic process?" but she didn't understand it.

Suddenly Patsy heard an alarming statement: "When you only have the title leader by virtue of election to a position and you are in a maintenance mode—doing little that's productive and reaching no new goals—there may be little reason for you to retain the position."

Patsy's lower lip began to quiver. She realized that she had not set the woods on fire with her commitment to missions, but give up her place on the WMU council? Surely not. "These women are my dearest friends," Patsy thought. She began to plan a luncheon for the bride-to-be daughter of another friend.

Mary Ellen Thomas wrapped her scarlet cape around her so that she was ever so cozy. The sterling silver family crest fastened the cape securely. She found herself drifting in and out; she needed a quick nap. Her head jerked up, however, when she heard Brenda say, "Pay your dues." However, she did not hear what Brenda said about paying dues. Mary Ellen was off on her own definition of paying dues.

"Like my mother before me, like my grandmother before her . . ." Mary Ellen silently pledged to herself and to her ancestors that she would be found faithful. A gentle snore followed her vow.

Anna looked at Patsy and Mary Ellen. "They will be with me forever," she thought. "So be it. They have potential and they both bring their own unique styles and background to the work: Patsy and her devoted friends, Mary Ellen and her family heritage. Perhaps it's time to find a dynamo to add to the duet. Who could it be, Lord?" Anna wondered. "Are You preparing her even now to join us here at Merrymount?"

Brenda began to conclude the retreat. "I'm handing each of you a dream sheet. Write down your dreams for next year."

Anna knew what she wanted to write. "And dear Lord," she prayed, "let this prayer of Amy Carmichael be my prayer, and maybe even the prayer for all of these women and the ones You are leading to us."

My vow: whatsoever Thou sayest unto me, by thy grace I will do it.

My constraint: Thy love, O Christ, my Lord.

My confidence: Thou art able to keep that which I have committed unto Thee.

My Joy: To do Thy will, O God.

My Discipline: That which I would not choose, but which Thy love appoints.

My Prayer: Conform my will to Thine.

My Motto: Love to live; live to love.

My Portion: The Lord is the portion of my inheritance.

Teach us, good Lord, to serve Thee as Thou deservest; to give and not to count the cost; to fight and not to heed the wounds; to toil and not to seek for rest, to labor and not to ask for any reward save that of knowing that we do Thy will, O Lord our God.*

Lead on!

---

*Elisabeth Elliot, *A Chance to Die: The Life and Legacy of Amy Carmichael* (Fleming H. Revell: New York, © 1987). Used by permission.

Teaching Plan

The preparation

Read the book and complete the learning activities for chapters 2 through 8.

Read the teaching plan and determine which actions will work best with your audience, how you should adapt the activities to meet their needs, and what items you should secure before the study.

Pray that you will lead the study with a servant heart and an awareness of the needs of the study participants. Pray that the study participants will discover how God would have them lead in their spheres of influence.

The plan

The study takes a chapter by chapter approach. Prepare an interest center that represents each chapter. Suggestions for items to include:

The Paradox of Servant Leadership—A pitcher, bowl, and towel

Uniquely Gifted for Servant Leadership—Gift bag with Scripture verses printed on strips

What Am I Doing Leading this Parade?—Balloons or a banner

Who Is that Leader in the Mirror?—Various sizes of mirrors

The Many Faces of Leadership—Photos of women and girls; magazines with recognized leaders on the covers

Who Will Follow in Your Footsteps?—Various styles of shoes

What Do You Mean, A Dynamic Process?—Action toys, pinwheels, etc.

Adapt the agenda to fit your needs. Note that a 2½-hour experience is required in order for participants to receive Church Study Course Credit.

Introductory Activity—Creating an image and discussion of roles (20 min.)

Chapter 1—Leadership review; brainstorming kinds of leadership (10 min.)

Chapters 2 and 3—Scripture search, discussion, and reflection (20 min.)

Chapter 4—True/False quiz, guided reflection (15 min.)

Chapter 5—Mirror game with partners, discussion of images (15 min.)

Chapter 6—Small group discussions (15 min.)

Chapter 7—Small group presentations (20 min.)

Chapter 8—Lecture with strip posters (15 min.)

Chapter 9—Leadership review; scripted testimonies from chapter (15 min.)

Concluding Activity—Dream sheets and commissioning prayer (5 min.)

The procedures

Introductory Activity—As participants enter the room, direct them to one of three work areas you've designated for producing: (1) a billboard; (2) a radio spot; or (3) a TV commercial. Instruct the groups at each area to work together to determine a promotional message about WMU and missions education. Provide paper and markers for the billboard team, a cassette and player for the radio team, and a video camera (if available) for the TV team. (If a camera and VCR are not available, have participants plan to present their spot "live.")

Allow 10 minutes for the discussions. Interrupt the planning and inform participants that they have been working as a team and now you want to discuss the process. Discuss responses to the following questions: Who took the lead in the group and why? Who seemed to be hesitant to lead but willingly followed? What gifts were evident among the participants?

Introduce the book *With a Servant Heart* and the authors using information from the introduction.

Chapter 1—Prior to the study, enlist women to represent the women whose names appear in italics in the first chapter. Arrange the room as though the women are participating in a pageant. As you introduce each character and describe her situation, the enlisted woman should walk along the stage area and assume some of her character's personality and mannerisms. Ask participants to brainstorm other kinds of WMU leadership and discuss responses.

Chapter 2 and 3—Refer to the interest center and the pitcher, bowl, and wash cloths. Ask what Scripture passage the center illustrates. Distribute wash cloths on which the Scripture references from chapter 2 have been pinned. As you present the information in chapter 2, ask holders of the cloths to read aloud when called on. Present the eight italicized statements from "What Does a Leader Do?" on page 15, and ask participants to offer biblical models that exemplify the statements. Note models mentioned in the text.

Segue into a discussion of chapter 3 by underscoring that each model identified was uniquely gifted by God. Call attention to the gift bag in the interest center. Distribute strips of paper from the bag on which you have previously written these selected verses from the chapter: Isaiah 49:15; Numbers 11:11-12; Isaiah 46:3; Isaiah 66:13; Hosea 11:3-4; Matthew 6:28-30; Matthew 23:37; Psalm 17:9; Psalm 61:4. Ask those who receive strips to read the verses aloud. Ask participants: What images do these verses bring to mind? Discuss the statement from page 15: "Women can bring their inherent nurturing gifts and concerns for relationships to servant leadership."

List the women from the Bible identified on pages 17-18. After a description of each, ask participants with which woman they identify most.

Chapter 4—Refer to the balloons in the interest center and introduce the chapter title. Distribute paper and pencils. Read aloud each statement of the True/False quiz and ask participants to respond on paper. Then review each statement with details from the chapter and encourage discussion. Present the information from "Focus on People" and "Focus on Tasks." Invite participants to fill in the blanks in the statements with names of leaders they know.

Chapter 5—Ask participants to select a partner. Review the material from "The Way We Perceive Ourselves." Direct the women to become a mirror for their partners' inner selves. Ask each woman to describe to her partner what the mirror reveals. Review "The Way We Present Ourselves" and invite partners to symbolically hold the mirror for each other as each participant notes what she can do to improve or strengthen her image. Refer to the billboard, radio spot, and TV commercial on which participants worked. Ask what positive points they would stress when promoting WMU and what WMU needs to do to improve the way it is presented to the church.

Ask participants to close their eyes and imagine a mirror that can reflect their everyday lives. Guide women to examine the reflection by using the questions included in "The Way We Perform Our Task."

Chapter 6—Refer to the photographs of leaders in the interest center. Note which models from the chapter are represented in the photos. Provide a brief description of each "face" of leadership. Ask participants to form small groups according to model with which they identify. Provide each group a copy of the book with pages marked which describe the model. Ask participants to scan the material and discuss responses to Study Question 3.

Chapter 7—Remain in small groups. Note the shoes included in the interest center. Ask participants to share the name of one woman who nurtured them and whose shoes they have tried to fill. Assign each group one of the sections of the chapter. (Do not assign the introductory remarks, but instead, ask two groups to review the material in "Enlist the Right People.") Ask them to prepare a presentation of the material using a method appropriate for their identified model of leadership (nurturer, mentor, administrator, etc.). Allow participants to present the material.

Chapter 8—Return to the large group. Present the information from this chapter as a lecture with strip posters of the boldface statements. Ask participants to respond to the Study Questions.

Chapter 9—Introduce again the characters first mentioned in chapter 1 by presenting another Leadership review. Change the format by allowing the character to pause at center stage and read or present dramatically her testimony (which you have previously scripted using the material from chap. 9).

Concluding Activity—Explain that in the book the characters from the Leadership review participate in a similar study and are asked to prepare dream sheets for the next year. Distribute blank paper and ask participants to do the same. After several minutes of reflection, invite participants to join you in a commissioning prayer. Copy the prayer on page 82 and 83 onto an overhead cell, poster, or flipchart. Mark the italicized portion for the women to read aloud. You should provide the response. Read the final statement together.